C.G. Jung in the Humanities

Susan Rowland

C.G. Jung in the Humanities

Taking the Soul's Path

Susan Rowland

Spring Journal Books
New Orleans, Louisiana

Published by
Spring Journal, Inc.
627 Ursulines Street #7
New Orleans, Louisiana 70116
Tel.: (504) 524-5117
www.springjournalandbooks.com

Cover design: Northern Cartographic
Typesetting: Michael Caplan

Printed in Canada
Text printed on acid-free paper

ISBN 978-1-935528-02-9
Library of Congress Cataloging-in-Publication Data Pending

Contents

To Joel Weishaus

for the inspiration

and for the Green Man

Acknowledgements

I want to thank some of the many people who were important in making this book happen. First of all, I honor Nancy Cater as a remarkable and imaginative publisher whose dedication merits lasting recognition. I also want to thank Michael Caplan for some dedicated and heroic copy-editing.

To my family, the Rowlands: thank you Mary, Cathy, John, Becca, Thomas, and Emma, especially for your support in the last six months of preparation of this book, which coincided with a difficult period in my life. Gratitude is due to kind and sympathetic friends, Wendy Pank, Christine Saunders, Margaret Erskine, Ailsa Montagu, Leslie Gardner, Lucy Huskinson, and Don Fredericksen.

Particular friends and colleagues contributed valuable essences to this book through generous conversations, excellent glasses of wine, and thoughtful hospitality. Among these are Jean Kirsch, Ginette Paris, Robert Romanyshyn, Robert Segal, Julia Paton, Roger Brooke, and Blake Burleson. I additionally must mention the patience of my friends at Greenwich University, notably John Williams, Justine Baillie, Jenny Bavidge, Pippa Guard, and Peter Humm. Significant contributions to this book were make by the various Literary Theory classes of 2008/2010. Special thanks to Laura, Lauren, Holly, Stacey, Luke, Victoria, Anna, Amelia, Yetunde, Sarah-Louise, and Charlie.

Lastly, I acknowledge the lasting inspiration of the poet, the late Edmund Cusick (1962-2007), whose powerful and evocative work in *Ice Maidens* (2006), is a lasting testament to the power of the imagination. From him and his wife, Christina Cusick, the light of friendship still shines.

Getting Started with Jung

*... [F]or in all chaos there is a cosmos,
in all disorder a secret order ...*
—C. G. JUNG [1]

*All key terms used in this chapter are written in **bold** and additional definitions can be found in the Glossary.*

Why You Should Read this Book

C. G. Jung in the Humanities: Taking the Soul's Path offers a new way of looking at the twenty-first century. It does so in three broad directions that take Jung and the humanities into different territory.

In the first place, whereas Jung is usually considered a writer *about* the imagination, myth, symbolism, poetics, literature, etc., this book shows him also as a writer *of* the imagination, myth, symbolism, poetics, and literature. Jung is a *creative* writer; an artist of the soul.

The second direction concerns the question of *why* Jung wrote as he did. Most people came to him for therapy because nothing in their lives seemed to have meaning. On a bigger scale, in a time directly touched by two world wars, Jung believed modern warfare, characterized by barbed wire and poison gas, to be the consequence of a psychological crisis. Jung held that the modern Western world was sick because it had excluded so much that seemed "other." So Jung as a writer tries to address the long marginalization of this psychic Other, summoning into his texts what has haunted modernity as "the feminine," the body, nature, myth, and the unconscious. His works become spaces where the human sciences, *the humanities*, find a new breath of being.

Finally, to read Jung is to witness a great quest to heal modernity by re-balancing the founding myths of consciousness. Western modernity was built upon a Christian religion that privileges separation, duality, and rationality as the expression of a Sky Father myth. Here, God is male *because* he separates himself from his "other," an Other who comes to represent the feminine and ultimately "Nature" (as created by him). Made first, "man" models himself upon God as transcendent and separate; woman is made *from* him, and so is culturally Other.

In such a myth, consciousness is structured on a model of rationality through division and exclusion, as I shall show. This myth has dominated modernity, mainly by suppressing an older myth based upon Nature herself as sacred. The Earth Mother is a Goddess, but not exclusively female because she contains all potentialities within her fertile body. She gives birth to women and men, offering consciousness based upon eros, body, and connection. While Christianity managed to retain a few elements of the Earth Mother myth in the figure of the Virgin Mary, Mother of God, the two *equally necessary* founding myths became severely unbalanced. As a consequence, the planet is being depleted, and epidemics of psychological distress rage on.

The humanities are one of the few spaces where Earth Mother qualities of relating and being are able to grow. In the arts, in symbolism, in new material forms of culture like film, in the growth of ecology and more Earth-centered forms of knowledge, Jung's efforts to wrench modern life away from one-sidedness echo loudly. *C.G. Jung in the Humanities* is about the rebirth of psychic life. It explores how his work renews the humanities and liberates the true nature of their creations as "creatures" inhabiting the human soul.

Jung and this Book

What is distinctive about C.G. Jung is that he took seriously the way our minds do not always make sense and our inner being is not always under our control. One way to represent this realization is to divide mental being, the psyche, into a *conscious* or knowable aspect, and an *unconscious* or unpredictable and partly unknowable realm. Jung devoted his life as therapist, writer, and cultural analyst to the consequences of accepting this mystery in ourselves.

Like Sigmund Freud, Jung developed a way of working with individual patients that he called (to distinguish it from Freudian psychoanalysis) "analytical psychology." Yet Jung's importance today also resides in his daring and experimental researches in culture, religion, science, and philosophy. This book will look at Jung's thinking in the context of modern debates about the self and society. It will place Jung's work in relation to the humanities, the arts, developing ideas of myth, changing scientific paradigms, and our connection to nature and the cosmos. For Jung's quest into the unknown part of the human being may open up a better road into the future.

Chapter 1 is devoted to exploring the theories of Jung about our psychological lives. For Jung, theory is not simply a matter of abstract intellectual forms making a satisfying picture of the mind; part of what is unique and valuable in Jungian psychology is his sense of the peculiarities inherent in studying the mental realm. He realized that psychology is a special discipline in that the *object* of knowledge, the psyche, is also the *means* of knowledge. The investigating tool is turned upon itself. Hence Jung's admission of the "personal factor" in making meaning.

Conditioning the personal are the cultural patterns that impinge both creatively and restrictively upon the individual. Jung's decision to make the cultural aspect of modern life a significant source for his work will be considered in Chapter 2. For now we might take note of Jung accepting the personal and subjective within his practice, which is marked by his distinction of two types of unconscious: the personal, pertaining to an individual's repressed material organized through the Oedipus complex (see below for **Oedipus complex**); and the collective, containing the inherited deposits of meaning-making from the history of humankind. This characteristic pivot between personal and collective is enshrined in the different metaphors used to frame the Jungian psyche: map, model, quest, myth, etc.

Before discussing these theoretical concerns, a dip into Jung's early career will reveal something of the doctor as experimental researcher.

Early Years: Experiments in Word Association

In December 1900, C.G. Jung, newly qualified as a physician, began work at the famous Burghölzli Mental Hospital, under the direction of Dr. Eugen Bleuler (1857-1939). Jung soon became involved in the first research to earn him professional recognition: word association experiments conducted with Franz Riklin, Sr.[2] Starting with Sigmund Freud's definition of "free association," in which the investigator offered words to the patient who responded as they wished, the procedure was refined to using one hundred words pre-selected for possible reactions. The subject was instructed not to free associate. Instead, he or she was to offer only the first word that came to mind in response.

Jung and Riklin made their own modification, focusing on the disturbances that erupted in the smooth running of the test. They discovered that the "difficulties" could be grouped by their origins in something upsetting, either in the patient's conscious life or repressed and unknown to the everyday self. Together with Riklin, Jung called these repressions "complexes," whether resulting from known or unknown distress.

The professional research atmosphere of the Burghölzli would not, for Jung, prove a barrier to the development of personal complications. In 1904, for example, Jung began to treat a young Russian woman, Sabina Spielrein. Although she left the hospital the following year, she and the now-married Jung continued a passionate relationship until she gained her medical degree and left the area in 1911. In 1905, when Jung's wife, Emma, became distressed by his interest in women patients, he asked her to take the word association test. Unsurprisingly, it showed the anxieties of a married woman who has become pregnant just when she wanted to be free to be more active in her husband's life, leaving her role as Jung's assistant to be filled by Sabina Spielrein and later by another ex-patient, Toni Wolff.

In January 1907, Jung himself took the word association test. Having turned the glass on the researcher, not only Jung's personal life but also his *unknown life* became part of the terrain of Jungian psychology. Crucially, Jung revealed tensions over money and over the possibility of divorce, as well as strong sexual excitement that seemed to point to Sabina Spielrein.[3] This sense of Jung as marked by an inner feminine figure who was not his wife is later inscribed in his theory as the **anima**, a psychic or dream character corresponding to the inner feminine soul of a man.

In his autobiography, composed with Aniela Jaffe, *Memories, Dreams, Reflections*,[4] Jung describes his discovery of the unconscious, beginning with visionary experiences in childhood. Part of his unique gift was to be able to reconcile the personal, the occult, and the culture of hospital research in a way that offered coherence to the modern man. Perhaps his lapses into misogyny on gender issues (see Chapter 6) are mitigated by his revelation of the power of the feminine: "She" is a creative force so independent and willful that it defeats his rationalizing theory about her.

The Importance of the Unconscious in Jungian Psychology

Jung's word association test as his own subject shows the conscious mind overwhelmed by an "unconscious feminine" associated with an actual woman. From such early experiments, Jung came to regard the unconscious as of defining importance to the psyche.

According to Jung, the word or concept **unconscious** has no essential content. We can know nothing certain about it. Statements about the unconscious cannot be tested for truth, Jung asserts.[5] Indeed, if the unconscious exists, it is not only unknowable in itself, it undermines all other secure forms of knowledge. For if we have this unknowable space, this mysterious energy living inside, then how can we be sure that we know anything else? After all, we cannot be sure what effect the unconscious is having on how our minds work and our criteria for truth.[6]

Of course, in order to propose that the unconscious undermines rational certainty in knowledge of all kinds, Jung had to first of all establish its influence. If the unconscious is a small dull spot in the mind then it will not possess the hypnotic powers affecting personality, ideas, and culture that Jung attributes to it. So for Jung, the unconscious is *autonomous*—it has agency and even designs upon the conscious part of being.[7] Moreover, the unconscious is *creative* in its own right.[8] It uses this creativity to lure consciousness into an ongoing relationship, as I shall show.

With all its inexhaustible fertility, the unconscious refuses to be limited by definitions. So it provides no "unifying principle," no point of origin or goal like those by which other intellectual disciplines can be ranked.[9] Unlike the Freudian unconscious, the Jungian unconscious neither privileges sexuality, nor science, nor art, nor history, nor biological evolution as the most *authentic* knowledge. The unconscious is always a creative challenge to what we know, not a means of reinforcing it.

Finally, the unconscious makes a demand upon *writing*. How is it possible to write of something that is unknowable, yet everywhere a living reality, a pulsing shaping energy behind the known world? How is it possible to evoke the quality of dreams (those visitors from the unconscious) in psychology, which is by definition *psyche-logos*, words of psyche? What Jung does in the face of this impossible task is to incorporate multiplicity into his writing. His work both respects boundaries and overleaps them. He invites the unconscious figures in the psyche to "in-spirit," that is, to *inspire* his pen. He also looks outwards into his world, and invites ghosts of the psyche from the past to spin him a tale.

Roger Brooke, who has written expertly on Jung and phenomenology, describes his development of terminology this way:

> Jung's language—shadow, *anima*, soul, spirit, *puer*, the great mother, trickster, and hero—and his use of alchemical and mythic imagery are explicitly an attempt to speak a psychological language not yet torn from its prerenaissance experiential roots.[10]

I am arguing that not only in developing specialized terms (anima, shadow, etc.; see below), but in the very texture of the writing, Jung invokes and makes a home for unconscious creativity. In 1933, he published a book of essays in English, *Modern Man in Search of a Soul*. Within the space of two pages he offers two metaphors for understanding the unconscious: it is a two-million-year-old human being; no, it is an endless sea of flowing images.[11] To write about the psyche as a mystery entails both a failure of language and, for Jung, an artistic departure into the subtle realm of metaphors.

Ultimately, Jung's writing offers an attempt to enlist the ungovernable energies of the psyche to make a viable framework for healing. Healing is addressed to himself, his patients, and even society. A framework in this sense is a metaphor that impacts upon the psyche: *how* you approach the mixture of unconscious and conscious energies affects *what* you see. After all, the *organ of perception* is also the *matter* that is perceived.

Jung's metaphors, frameworks, and conceptual terms such as anima, shadow, etc., are part of the struggle of language to represent an unrepresentable psyche, metaphors that *both represent and shape psychic reality*. So Jung's language retains metaphoric status in its acknowledgement of the essential mystery. Among Jung's favorite metaphorical frameworks are notions of map, model, quest, and the alchemical "work against nature."

Jungian Psychology as a Map

A spatial metaphor for the inner world is common, and indeed hard to give up as my use of "inner world" indicates. The term **psyche** stands for the entire extent of the phenomena of conscious and unconscious, but "psyche" does suggest a limit, binding the psychic to *inside* the human being. Jung essentially adhered to the philosopher Descartes' insistence upon a strict division between subject and object, self and world. On the other hand, his work contained intimations of subjectivity deriving from an ensouled world *outside*. Here we have a typical pattern of Jung's urge to transcend the boundaries of the reality of his own era. We will see how he manages this feat later.

The psyche **dreams**. One of the most ubiquitous creative products of the unconscious is the dream. Dreams are the direct expressions of the unconscious[12]; they are not of secondary reality to some concealed desire. Dreams are not in code and have no message behind them; however enigmatic, however shocking, however erotic, dreams should be attended to on their own terms. The one way to respect dreams is to stick to the dream images.[13] The dream itself, enshrined in its own *image-ination*, may lead the way to its own significance.

Indeed the real truth of a dream might not ever be expressible in words. A dream's images are more important than words, even healing words, because they are the native art of the unknowable unconscious. Only by valuing the dream's images over explanatory words can the real importance of unconscious energy be preserved. As I will show, freeing the unconscious to soak up the *matter* of the psyche is necessary because it is the unknown creative part of the mind that houses healing potential.

Consequently, if dreams are more significant than verbal explanations, they also challenge the validity of theory. Jung is acutely aware of epistemology, of ways of assessing or valuing knowledge. He says that if a dream baffles the presuppositions of a doctor, then it is the presuppositions that have to go. The reader of dreams ought to be prepared to construct a new theory for each dream.[14] Perhaps fortunately for the practicalities of psychotherapy, he does admit the necessity for some consistent theory in order to produce intelligible outcomes.[15]

In practice, Jung's consistent theory grants superior significance to the dream as visitor from the sublime unconscious. Jung never relinquishes his intellectual starting point: the unknowability and creativity of the unconscious. It is the one proposition that cannot be removed from Jungian psychology or deconstructed, in part because the unknown psyche can challenge every idea but that of its own potency.

As transmissions from the creative unconscious, dreams are images from a higher realm which *happen* to the **ego**, another spatially imagined concept. Jung accepted the function of Freud's **Oedipus complex**, whereby the ego forms in infancy via the repression of forbidden desires for the mother. On the other hand, he never accepted the importance Freud attributed to it. Rather, Jung chose to prioritize the autonomy and creativity of the unconscious, first manifested in early childhood as the birth of the ego from the depths of the psyche. Here the unconscious is the womb of the Great Mother. For Jung, the Oedipal mother is real, and based on fantasies about the actual woman; yet the creative unconscious, in the role of "mother" to the ego, is far more significant in a person's development.

From time to time, Jung described the ego as a "complex," consisting of those aspects of consciousness grounded in the body.[16] Thus he suggests a key role for bodily boundaries just as Freud does. Similarly, the ego is a function; it centers and unifies consciousness.[17] By drawing consciousness into being, the ego enables the dualistic division of the psyche into conscious and unconscious. Jung has a startlingly geographical depiction of the erupting potentials for psychic self-knowledge.

Gleaming islands, indeed whole continents can still add themselves to our modern consciousness.[18]

The creation of consciousness is a never-finished work of truly Herculean effort. It raises land from the sea of unbeing to be freshly trod by a colonizing ego. And, of course, to follow the geographical metaphor is to envisage the fires of undersea volcanoes, the powerhouse energies of the creative unconscious. Early in his career Jung deduced that unconscious complexes influence behavior, which he then called "dominants." Later he settled upon the term **archetypes**, to signify inherited creative potentials for certain sorts of images and meaning.

Archetypes are not *inherited* images or ideas, nor are they inborn meanings or figures ready to sprout under the right stimulus. Archetypes have no form in themselves. They may even have no existence under normal definitions. Jung called the archetype a "hypothesis" to account for the way the human psyche makes similar images in dreams and art across cultures and throughout history. This enabled Jung to assume a human commonality of psychic energies, devoted to manifesting the creativity of the whole person.

Only **archetypal images**, not the hypothetical and ultimately unrepresentable archetypes-in-themselves, have form. They are the joint offspring of the hypothetical archetype and the social world of the person. Archetypal imagery is cultural and bodily, while not being *determined* by culture or body. Consequently, archetypes are our collective humanness, what Jung called the **collective unconscious**.

Unsurprisingly, the archetype, however unprovable a hypothesis and unrepresentable in itself, shares and embodies Jung's notion of the unconscious as sublime, as signifying an ultimately unrepresentable potential. Archetypal images frequently come fringed with numinosity, that is, with spirituality, religious resonance, or awe. Since these images are the closest we can come to the heart of the archetype (although inevitably colored by social experience), the archetypal images *are* the meaning. Like dream images (which are archetypal), they cannot be accurately translated into words or be displaced by them.[19] Moreover, the images are limitless as to their possible shape and dimensions.

Jung believed that archetypes were like inner guardians, like Greek and Roman gods, reconceived as typical patterns of behavior. So he would discuss a "mother" or a "hero" archetype. Yet the mother archetype is not restricted to the form of a woman. "She" can show her dark side as an evil, devouring dragon. Or she can be heavenly as a goddess, primeval as a snake, or elementally sheltering as a cave.

The complexity of the notion of archetypes and archetypal images fired Jung throughout his career. In particular, it drove him to seek out cultural and historical traditions that might express and validate these mysterious and evocative symbols. For example, the researcher of word associations discovered disturbances he called "complexes." Later he reserved the word "complexes" for repressed personal material such as interested Freud. Archetypal images, by contrast, came to stand for psychic activity that had never been repressed, that was striving through the darkness for expression.

Sounding like a laboratory scientist, Jung once described archetypes as a saturated solution of crystals.[20] The solution requires the stimulus of the embodiment of the psyche to give it the heat to crystallize into the archetypal image. Interestingly, Jung sticks to the metaphor of mother here: the crystalline solution is a matrix of images and the intimation of meaning. Indeed it is a "mother" of infinite possibilities.

Typically, Jung's metaphor of mother is not quite a metaphor. Let us recall the ego's birth from the autonomous, active unconscious. Here in the creative depths of psyche is the primal drive behind the child's separation from the mother through the discovery of bodily boundaries. Whereas some theories would see the unconscious as a realm *deriving* from the mother's body, Jungian psychology reverses the priorities of being. While the body and its psychic boundaries are independent in relation to the person, for Jung the most *fundamental* mother is the collective unconscious itself.

Through his study of alchemy, Jung discovered his largest and most cosmic spatial vision: the archetypal unconscious is a heaven full of stars.[21] Jung is hinting here that the unconscious is a many-eyed being, or like multiple glowing fish eyes in deep waters.[22] Through archetypes, we possess many potential selves, for these numinous energies are partial, embryonic consciousnesses reaching out to us for embodiment in the world. Such a vision suggests that the self, or conscious being, is multiple. As I will show later, Jung had ways of modifying this radical plurality.

Jungian Psychology as a Model

The previous section showed that Jung made use of spatial metaphors for the psyche, as well as suggesting that he drew upon different cultural legacies in the challenge of centering his writing on something ultimately mysterious. In addition to spatial dimensions, Jung intimated that the psyche was dynamically related to time. The psyche is always cultural in that culture colors what is manifested, yet it is not limited to culture and neither are we. One way in which the psyche can express its otherness to the daylight world of conscious social being is to draw upon symbols of an-Other time, as I will discuss below.

Adding a characteristic pragmatism to this fascination with time gives us Jung's description of his psychology as a "model": a set of interlocking ideas to be judged on how they *work* to help understand embodied existence in time. He said that his "model" was not an assertion of absolute truth; it was merely a way of observing and intervening in the psyche.[23] As David Tacey perceptively remarks, we should think of his key terms as "processes" as well as "things."[24]

Another way is to divide Jungian terminology into his own two categories of **signs** and **symbols**. Signs are images and words that stand for a known quality or thing, and mainly signify conscious thought. Symbols, on the other hand, direct us to the unknown, numinous unconscious for their true reality. So taking Jung's concepts like the "**shadow**" in a way that stresses their intelligibility turns them into known "things" and "signs." Yet if Jung's key terms do refer to the collective unconscious, then we ought to keep in mind that they are also hypothetical models, "processes," and symbols.

This sense of a living mystery embedded in Jungian language is apparent in another term shared with Freud, yet again used very differently by Jung. **Libido** is, for Freud, psychic sexual energy. Jung, typically, liberated the word from too much conscious definition; *his* libido merely stands for psychic energy in all its mutable shape-shifting properties. Of course, psychic energy may occur as sexuality at a particular moment in a person's life. Yet for Jung, libido cannot be restricted to being a mere "sign" of the sexual origins of the self, for our origins lie deep in the numinous dreamland of being.

The **shadow** is, on the one hand, a wonderfully economic expression for the tendency of the unconscious to grip the ego through opposition or compensation. The shadow as "thing" is monstrous, for it is what we have no desire to be. Usually evil, the shadow cannot even be fully grasped as inner darkness, for a bad ego or evil person may possess a lighter shadow. What the shadow heralds is the arrival of moral problems: psychic life demands to be lived, and the shadow, carrying those parts of ourselves we do not approve of, strives for expression even against the conscious will. [25]

As a process, the shadow represents frustration and defeat, usually in darkness. But it is essential that we come to terms with the shadow, the inner, demon, for our vitality depends upon it. This means renouncing the idea that all evil is "outside" us. To ignore the inner shadow is to permit the dark energy to strengthen. Persons and even nations who deny the archetypal dynamism of the shadow will find their conscious capacities weakening. Eventually the enfeebled ego is washed away by black currents; sanity and even civilization are broken.

Gender is a process between conscious and unconscious as well. Here Jung is not straightforward. From the point of view of the everyday world, he was *essentialist* regarding gender because he believed that men and women were born, not made, that sexed bodies have "natural" and biologically-influenced gender roles. On the other hand, the Jungian universe places the creative unconscious as a source of meaning above all others. So gender is also a sign of the Other as spiritual or numinous. By encountering potent images of the opposite gender, we engage in creative transformation as we meet the Otherness of the unconscious. This clash between conservative ego and imaginative vision is played out in Jung's writings, where misogynist remarks are entwined with radical challenges to the notion of gender as a simple duality. No other aspect of Jung's thought has provoked more debate and revision. (See Chapter 6, and Further Reading, below.)

For Jung, although men have a masculine psyche and women a feminine psyche, both sexes also have a powerfully gendered Other in their unconscious. Indeed, the other gender is the main gateway to the unconscious for both sexes. Here gender as a path to the soul is literal, in that relationships with the opposite gender become the means of psychically bonding with the Other within. In fact, gender as erotic relationship is literal *and* metaphorical: the Other within is the path to embracing the other without, and vice versa. Just as we may discover our own shadow in a hated person because we have unconsciously projected our dark energy onto them, so do we reach out to the other gender for what we have not integrated within ourselves. We find our inner otherness and creativity in the women and men around us.

A male's unconscious feminine is called the **anima**; a woman's inner masculine is the **animus**. Here is the radical germ in Jung's gendering. For our gendered being is an on-going creative process with the Other, a process connected to gender in the world, *but not limited by it*. Nothing can limit the creativity of the unconscious, so even the most patriarchal societies cannot control the lived experience of feminine and masculine. The unconscious will always supersede and soften stereotypes as part of its unbreakable romance with the ego.

Gender is, therefore, an opening into the unconscious. Jung gives an example of this when he recalls a woman's voice that spoke spontaneously to him in his imagination during a time of great psychic distress.[26] This episode testifies to the psychic potency of gender as it summons unfathomable depths.

Anima and animus as processes and symbols have a lot to offer gender theory. Unfortunately, Jung's thoughts on gender are sometimes also simplifications. The anima too often dwindles to banality, or is characterized as a nagging woman. However, for all her evident inferiorities, the anima retains the psychic potential to return the man to the business of life,[27] while the animus is rarely described positively. Too frequently the animus is criticized for inspiring women with rootless "opinions" and "animosity" towards men.[28] Only occasionally does Jung concede that the animus is not all bad news. Thus one problem with his writings on anima and animus is the switch from the imaginative quality of symbols to the transparency of signs. Treating symbols as signs indicates the attempt to fix the meaning of what, by its psychic nature, is unfixable.

A similar problem is generated by two other key words, also gendered: **logos** and **eros**. Logos, for Jung, is associated with the Father, and signifies abstract thought, characterized by discrimination and separation. Eros, associated with the Mother, stands for connection, body, and feeling. Jung makes these associations because it is simply "so" that women tend to be more eros-oriented and men more devoted to logos.[29] On the one hand, Jung is careful to insist upon logos and eros merely as complementary functions not necessarily assigned to separate genders, yet he frequently lapses into the banality of social prejudice, saying, for example, that logos in a woman is often a "regrettable accident."[30] Chapter 6 on gender and power will look further at the polarization of Jung's thoughts on gender, from misogynist remarks to sublime visions.

Jungian psychology's most far-reaching technique for making the psyche comprehensible, for rescuing order from chaos, is to use oppositions. Jung structures his model of the psyche in oppositional or complementary pairs. From ego versus shadow, we can see gender in opposing pairs as masculine animus facing feminine ego, or feminine ego with typical eros functions in her consciousness discovering logos in her unconscious, etc. Other oppositional pairs that seek reconciliation include **types** of people. Jung coined the well known terms *extraversion* and *introversion*, the former indicating those who turn outwards to human society for psychological growth, in contrast to the latter who focus on the inner world.

What is often *implicit* in Jung's oppositions is an emphasis upon process. By reading the model *symbolically*, we see these opposites begin to break down and interact creatively in the psyche. In modern terms, Jung's oppositions deconstruct; Jung proposes a *self-deconstructing psyche*.

Jung borrowed the ancient term **enantiodromia** to signify that opposites would sometimes "go into reverse," change places. Jung also developed the concept of the **transcendent function** to indicate a process of resolving intolerable conflicts or opposing energies. If two mutually exclusive psychological states collide with no obvious way to ease the tension, then a third uniting entity may arise from the creative unconscious. This is usually a powerful symbol able to resolve and heal the conflict. Generating a third thing to heal the binary split *is* the transcendent function. As the name suggests, it is a higher energy coming to the aid of an unbearable conflict. In the very mysteries of the Jungian symbol, is a flowering that captivates and tames the pain of the conflict.

Jung also liked to expand his dualist preference to patterns of four, *quaternities*. Beyond introversion and extraversion, he developed a scheme including four further types: thinking, feeling (valuing), intuition, and sensation. Jung called these function-types. They vary in intensity and competence between individuals, as well as within them, i.e., the ego may adhere to one type while the unconscious is devoted to another. The type hidden in the unconscious is the underdeveloped or, in Jung's terminology, *inferior* function, which needs to be brought into the light so that its oppositional or compensatory aspects can be fully realized.

Regarding Jungian keywords as processes as well as things, as symbols as well as signs, begins to give a sense of the psyche as an entity in time as well as in space. To look more closely at the role of time and space, I am going to consider Jungian psychology as a special kind of a journey: a quest.

Jungian Psychology as a Quest

Jungian psychology is a quest because it envisions psychic life as a journey with a goal. Jung believed that the psyche is intrinsically *teleological*, that is, oriented towards some future goal or significance. Jung called that goal the **Self** (or sometimes **self**; this book will use Self for the specifically Jungian term). Our deepest psychic energies are not subject to the conscious will. They direct us to forge a relationship with numinous phenomena in the unconscious. This inner powerhouse, this inner star or sun, will even take the initiative and seek out a reluctant ego. Such unconscious directedness is the Self because it is the truest core of our being. Compared to the Self in the unconscious, the ego is a frail cultural construction, fit only to be the Self's satellite. The Self is the center of being, and is discovered in the unconscious. It nurtures and promotes the deconstructive tendencies so that it may imbue the psyche with ultimate order out of its chaos.

The goal of the psychic quest throughout life is to realize—to *make real*—the Self as the heart of being. The Jungian psyche is thus teleological, goal-oriented, and embraces paradox. For the Self is portrayed as an archetype in the unconscious, one capable of becoming the supreme source of centering and order.

Yet the Self is not "just" in the unconscious, it is also the complete wholeness of being. Part of psychic mystery is that the Self includes within its limits both ego consciousness and the creative unconscious, yet at the same time, the Self is in some sense *limitless* because the limits of the unconscious cannot be known. Here the notion of the Self floods outward into the physical and even the metaphysical world. For Jung, Self becomes a mode of exploring the many ways the psyche has of *seeking home* in body, intimate relationships, culture, and cosmos.

In these senses, the Self is spatial and temporal. It is the goal and the sense of wholeness the goal promises. It is a dimly intuited Grail on a life quest, and it is the totality of experience on the way to that destination. The Self is also the world coming forth alive into our subjectivity; our experience of time and space creatively combined. Chapter 4, on myth and history, will take further some of these notions of the psyche as realized in time and place.

Jung found two images of the Self particularly significant. One was the mandala, a complex circular formation appearing in many mythologies, which he also detected in his patient's dreams. Encouraging patients to draw mandalas became the beginnings of Jungian art therapy. In the multiple possibilities and circularity of the mandala, Jung saw the plural nature of the unconscious, as well as an evocation of the archetypes as a star-filled heaven brought into a one-ness of order and harmony.

A second, even more striking image of the Self for Jung is the image of the Christian God or Jesus. Here we can see Jung's vision of a culturally engraved psyche. Centuries of monotheistic religion assume a place in shaping the Jungian quest for Self. Whether such religion itself grew out of psychological truth or in fact shaped it, Jung refuses to speculate. He insisted that his work remained psychological, not theological. Chapter 5 of this book will look at these contested areas.

For now, Jung's psychological belief was that religion had the responsibility to regulate individual and collective psyches through its symbols and rituals. He felt that his Christian religion had failed to maintain a vital contact with the deep selves of the population in the modern world. In that failure was born the new science of psychology, with a mission to re-connect the psyche or soul to the numinous within.

Given that the hypothesis of the unconscious posits nothing, as Jung insisted, he could fairly argue that his *Self as God-image in the psyche* posed no challenge to any particular religion. The Self is a node of psychic power without doctrinal content. It embraces all antitheses, is good and evil, feminine and masculine, divine and defiling. Jung offers the atheist the possibility of happily exploring spirituality in the Self, for this notion of the Self insists upon no separate reality of God beyond the psychic image. On the other hand, a person of faith, at least of monotheistic faith, can bring that faith and Jung's quest for Self together as the same story. The Self does not insist upon a transcendent God, meaning one apart from and above the real world. Yet the Self can co-exist with a belief in a divine reality not limited to the individual psyche.

To put it another way, Jung's quest for Self regards human life as a journey in search of inner meaning. It can also be fitted into a religious quest for a relationship with the supernatural. After all, the Self cannot be limited in any way, by physical boundary, by temporal period, or by any specific set of meanings. The Self is the transcendent function incarnated in Jungian writings. It is the figure that maps Jungian psychology onto the unknown.

Fascinatingly, this drive to map complexity and chaos into coherence by evoking the Self is met with contrary tendencies in Jung's work. For there is also a valuing of multiplicity in his ideas. Archetypes are many; they embed multiple possibilities into the psyche. They, too, can manifest as good and bad, masculine and feminine, human or animal, divine or demon, etc. So despite the singleness of the Self as goal, there remains the contrary possibility of a polytheistic or animistic psyche in the plurality of archetypes. Indeed, this deep tension in Jungian psychology, between the dominant "one-ness" and monotheism of Western heritage and an innate multiplicity or animism, will prove crucial later in this book.

For now there are two further key elements in the quest for individuality and authenticity. **Persona** stands for a mask of personality that is oriented towards the social and professional environment. The persona is a solidifying of personality, half-consciously sculpted for everyday life in the workplace and the street. We all need a persona. Yet we ought not to become so caught up in the persona that we cannot remove the mask. Those imprisoned in their social faces, their personas, are starved of the deep unconscious energies of true psychic health.

Individuation is Jung's name for the quest for Self. To be precise, the term means that the pro-active unconscious continually re-shapes our being throughout life. "Individuation" stands for the lifelong journey seeking psychic authenticity through ever more profound relationships with unconscious archetypal energies. By relating to the spiritual or numinous unknown, we become more and more what we have the potential to be, more *individual*. Individuation is not primarily about making the ego. Rather it is about the ego learning the greater intimations of being possible through the guiding stars (archetypes) within. These often direct us outwards to the world and to relationships.

Individuation has a goal, but no limits. After all, the unknowable domain beyond the ego cannot be mapped. So individuation is far from a selfish retreat into ego. It embraces the mysteries of the human heart in connecting to others.

Ultimately, individuation spills over what is commonly thought of as the division between self and world. Put another way, Jung's model, map, and theory, taken as *signs*, all appear to assume that the psyche is "inside" us and sometimes projected "outside" onto other people or aspects of the world. We are all individual subjects whose bodily boundaries incarnate a mental existence intrinsic to ourselves—subjects facing the world as object, as Descartes insisted. Yet Jung quested beyond the knowable and also offered his key ideas as *symbols*. As I will show in later chapters, he both upheld and unraveled the subject/object distinction. Now we need to look at the role of the **body** in relation with this active and autonomous psyche. The psyche lives with—and needs to relate to—the body, which provides another of the psyche's mysterious permeable boundaries. Instincts are those psychic energies that are driven by bodily needs and functions, yet instincts are not *only* the manifestations of bodily drives. As they shape psychic energy, they are themselves creatively affected by archetypal patterning. In fact, instincts and archetypes are of the same order: instincts are the bodily pole of archetypes, while archetypal images are produced in the psyche as the spiritual pole of bodily instinct.

Jung says that the creative psyche spiritualizes the body, while the body incarnates the spirit. Crucially, neither has priority. The body does not control or originate the psyche, while the psyche cannot subdue the body's needs. Body and psyche exist in a deconstructive relationship, continually re-making, re-imagining their liminal borderlines.

At one point Jung uses the helpful metaphor of the light spectrum to express the body-psyche continuum. At one end are the intensities of red radiance, suggesting blood and the needs of the body's instinctual energy. At the other end of the spectrum are the mystical violet glows of the archetypal image. He reminds us that both the functioning of our own bodies and the limits of our psyches are unfathomable to us. We cannot feel our own nervous system nor intuit how far the mind can reach.

Jung used the term "psychoid" for the place where body and archetype meet. Given his abiding interest in the relationship between matter and psyche, it is not surprising that his later work took the conjoining of matter and the psyche in an astonishing direction. For Jung was to take the notion of the individuation quest into a sense of active collaboration with matter and time as *animated*. Finding the inherited notion of a mechanical, spiritless universe untenable with his psychology, he pursued his sense of a world actively intervening in the psyche in an irrational yet ultimately meaningful way. He called this phenomenon **synchronicity**.

To Jung, synchronicity indicates "meaningful coincidences" where a psychic state corresponds to something in the outside world, *and yet* this coinciding does not seem to be caused in the usual material manner. Rather, the connection appears to be one of deep coherence. The "coincidence" is poetically meaningful and intimates some hidden pattern in reality.[31] Jung speculates that synchronistic events rest upon an archetypal base. Archetypes are dedicated to building human meaning through pattern, images, bodily impulses, spiritual intuitions, and eros modes of creative love for persons, culture, and cosmos.

Jung's most famous example of synchronistic experience comes from his practice as a therapist. A young woman who is "stuck" in her analysis recounts a dream of a golden scarab. At that very moment, Jung sees an insect trying to get in at the window. It proves to be a beetle of the scarab family. This "coincidence" of nature and psyche so strikes the patient that her inner creative sparks are at last released. The analysis finally begins to move productively.[32] Jung informs the reader that, archetypally, the scarab is an ancient rebirth symbol.

Another example of a synchronicity is the gathering of birds around the houses of the dying.[33] Yet such phenomena are not limited to non-human nature and psyche, and dreams and intuitions may synchronistically connect us to social life in ways untraceable to conscious stimuli. Moreover some synchronous events are not simultaneous; rather, they predict the future. These may indicate future catastrophes, such as dreams that predict the death of someone known or a presentiment of an accident. Jung argues that such examples are not strictly *synchronous*, that is, together in time; but they are *synchronistic*, since the relevant psychic or archetypal image appears in the present bearing a meaningful forward resonance. So synchronicity refers to meaningful coincidences separated from consciousness by space or time.[34]

Ultimately, Jung regards synchronicity as indicating that space and time are of the same nature. They are "probably" essentially the same.[35] So synchronicity is a form of acausal ordering or patterning in reality.[36] Its archetypal properties are inherent in the ordering, but it is not causal in any way. After all, archetypes are intrinsically creative and cannot be viewed mechanically. Rather Jung calls synchronicities "acts of creation in time" [37] (see Chapter 5).

Synchronicity is the spontaneous marriage of space, time, and psyche to produce meaning, significance, and image. An important development in Jung's work, later chapters of this book will explore the increasing relevance of synchronicity to the artistic, mythical, and scientific explorations of the twenty-first century.

Finally, we need to keep in mind the two factors required for something to be considered a synchronicity. First, there will be some kind of image from the unconscious, either directly erupting into consciousness or appearing indirectly as, for example, a dream of premonition. Second, there will be a coinciding objective situation, separated in space or time, with no causal link.[38] In such a way does Jung theorize the individuation quest. Psychic meaning and expansion of self are not only matters of mining the unconscious as imagined *within* the body. For those who are sensitive to the way the psyche reaches out to the world, there is a reciprocal embrace.

Jung's notion of synchronistic acts of creation in time is not limited to the individual. Instead, synchronicity is a fundamental reality, enfolding matter, space, time, and psyche in a meaningful living whole. Individuation is a quest, not just for the numinous goal, but for a mutual relationship of creativity with the world. So it is not surprising that Jung suggested that narrative and in particular those forms of storytelling associated with psychic growth were important stores of psychic health in culture. After all, what is synchronicity if it is not a psychology of magic?

Jungian Psychology as Narrative: Mythos and Logos

Because Jungian psychology seeks to express the inexpressible, Jung says that his psychology is a metaphor, one in a long historical series that in turn will be superseded.[39] He calls his work an attempt to acknowledge the unknowable dark impulse that wants to take form in the human world. In so doing, he likens himself to an artist or a dancer.[40] So in this chapter we have moved from the static to the dynamic, from map and model to journey and quest, from concepts as "thing" and sign to "process" and symbol.

In the quest metaphor, Jungian psychology becomes a transformational entity, reconceiving or rebirthing the world and the psyche as dynamically co-creative. Hence the quest infers *narrative* as the major form of Jungian psychological expression. To put it another way, the quest returns us to the ancient question of knowledge as mythos or logos.

To ancient Greeks such as Plato and Aristotle, mythos stands for the epic narratives of gods and heroes that frame and make possible Greek history, identity, and culture. These myths are expressions of psychic potential because they represent some kinds of being beyond normal human limitations. Logos, on the other hand, is the type of abstract, rational knowledge that is non-narrative, yet is ultimately dependent upon the myth. Plato famously resorted to a transcendent realm of perfect Forms, but his only way of positing such perfection was through a story. In his famous myth of the cave, imperfect man could only see reflections of the truth on the cave's walls.[41]

Gradually the Greeks came to prefer the reasoned order of logos in their philosophy and science to the unsettling possibilities of mythos. Christianity adopted the preference for making logos doctrine out of divine storytelling. This was followed by the Enlightenment's exaltation of reason, which accelerated the eclipse of mythos, as Laurence Coupe explains.[42]

These two types of knowledge, mythos and logos, will prove vital to the rest of this book. Here we can see not only Jung's explicit interest in myths, but even more daringly, the *extent to which his whole psychology opens itself to being a form of mythos*. Jung's psychology as mythos speaks to the infinite imaginative human possibilities only expressible as (individuation) stories.

Of course, Jung's writing is actually a mixture of mythos and logos. He is a logos thinker when he produces concepts and theory, and a mythos creator of stories and images, one who pays tribute to the inexpressible. Even more important than recognizing the simultaneous presence of mythos and logos in Jung's work is the vital relationship they form. For Jungian psychology arises from a dialogical relationship between mythos and logos. Here conceptual abstract knowledge exists *only* by virtue of relating to narrative openness, to permanent possibility. Vice versa, the narrative aspect of Jung's writing only gains comprehensibility by its reference to abstract logos concepts.

So on the one hand, Jung described his ideas as "personal myth," standing for his discovery of and struggles with his own unconscious narrative, from which he generated his ideas. Myths, he decided, were stories that both expressed and shaped the psyche: these stories trace and reconfigure the boundaries between social world and inner self.

Nevertheless, as we have seen, Jung also claimed logos for his psychology. He built concepts from the individuation narratives of his and others' lives, although he frequently admitted that abstract, conceptual logos represented just part of the truth. Only mythos—in the form of narrative, imaginative imagery, and symbols—is able to invoke the unknown energies of the soul.

I have suggested elsewhere that Jung's work is a dialogue of personal myth and grand theory.[43] Put another way, Jung gives us back mythos to soothe the loneliness of logos in comprehending humanity. The truth of logos is not enough; Jung insists also upon the boundless possibilities of mythos.

Jung: Practical Psychology, Experimental Writing

Jung worked a long professional life, seeing patients, training others to be Jungian analysts, and writing. His was an essentially practical psychology, not least because a pragmatic approach to what works took precedence over adherence to theory. To use the kind of religious language that Jung felt comfortable with, he was a shaman working with psychic powers as he found them, rather than a priest teaching a set creed.

Of course, the justification for this founding flexibility was the fundamental principle of the unknowable, protean unconscious. Such a principle displaces a search for some fixed, abstract "truth" in favor of a quest for numinous authenticity. So Jung's writing becomes experimental. It draws in cultural resources through anecdotes, fairy tales, beliefs, and practices from the past. So important is Jung's use of one historical phenomenon, alchemy, that it will become the major focus of Chapter 5. Jung's work negotiates and explores beyond the apparent boundary between psyche and nature; and Jung's work seeks out traces of the psyche in historical texts and rejuvenates their images and symbols for today.

Above all, Jung's experimental writing offers the rational grid of a dualistic psychology, *animated* by a dialogical tension with a plurality of voices and meanings. This particular dialogue of oneness with multiplicity is one of Jung's most important legacies for the twenty-first century. The next chapter will return to the question of Jung's experimental writing and look further at his own analysis of culture. What voices are liberated by writing that reaches out to the *whole* psyche? What do they have to say to today's fears and perplexities over the shadows of nature, of religious intolerance and weapons of mass destruction?

FURTHER READING

Deirdre Bair, *Jung: A Biography* (New York: Little, Brown, 2004).
The most recent, comprehensive and readable of the Jung biographies. This is a tour de force of scholarship and the biographer's art.

Roger Brooke, ed., *Pathways into the Jungian World: Phenomenology and Analytical Psychology* (London and New York: Routledge, 2000).
This important essay collection is a lucid re-thinking of the philosophical implications of Jungian thought.

James Hillman, *The Dream and the Underworld* (New York: Harper & Row. 1979).
Like Jung, the eminent analyst and scholar James Hillman takes the god-like creative power of the imagination seriously as a starting point. Here he delves into the diverse history of dream theory from Heraclitus to Jung and Freud, but his real topic is the underworld "Hades" that dreams reveal in us.

C.G. Jung, *The Collected Works of C. G. Jung* (CW), edited by Sir Herbert Read, Dr. Michael Fordham and Dr. Gerhard Adler, trans. R.F.C. Hull (London: Routledge, 1953; Princeton, NJ: Princeton University Press, 1991).
For the beginner, Jung's *Collected Works* are best to dip into for samples of his remarkable and challenging style. Except where a different publication is noted below, all references in this book are, by volume and paragraph number, to the above edition of the English text.

C.G. Jung, *Modern Man in Search of a Soul*, trans. W.S. Dell and Cary F. Baynes (London and New York: Routledge, 1933).
An early English translation, this essay collection contains some key ideas such as Jung's reading of non-Western cultures in "Archaic Man," art in "Psychology and Literature," and a number of pieces critical of modernity.

C.G. Jung, *Memories, Dreams, Reflections* (London: Fontana, 1963).
Jung's autobiography (with Aniela Jaffe) makes a very readable introduction to his ideas as well as his life.

R.K. Papadopoulos and G.S. Saayman, eds., *Jung in Modern Perspective:
The Master and his Legacy* (Great Britain: Prism Press, 1984/1991).
An invaluable collection of modern essays that contains an important
piece by Renos Papadopoulos, "Jung and the Concept of the Other,"
which explores for the first time Jung's renowned criticism of Freud as
employing what he called a "nothing but" psychology.

R.K. Papadopoulos, ed., *The Handbook of Jungian Psychology: Theory,
Practice and Applications* (New York: Routledge, 2006).
Mainly written by distinguished analysts, this vital new collection of
essays provides a good overview of developing theory, with a useful
section on contexts in religion and the arts.

Susan Rowland, *Jung: A Feminist Revision* (Oxford: Polity, 2002).
The book considers aspects of gender in Jung and the post-Jungians,
as well as offering some new research and examining the status of
"theory" in Jung.

Andrew Samuels, *Jung and the Post-Jungians* (London: Routledge &
Kegan Paul, 1985).
Andrew Samuels is an important figure in the development of multi-
disciplinary Jungian Studies out of clinical analytical psychology. This
book is a mapping of Jung's ideas and their relationship to psychotherapy and to other forms of knowledge.

Andrew Samuels, Bani Shorter and Fred Plaut, eds., *A Critical Dictionary
of Jungian Analysis* (London and New York: Routledge, 1986).
A real help in the further understanding of Jung's key terms, this
dictionary shows how they developed throughout different writings.

David Tacey, *How to Read Jung* (Great Britain: Granta, 2006).
Superb in its lucidity, this short book is a marvelous combination of
the accessible and the thought-provoking.

For More on Myth and Nature

Laurence Coupe, *Myth* (London and New York: Routledge, 1997).
  About to be re-issued with excellent content on Jung, Coupe's clear and exciting overview of myth is indispensable.

Laurence Coupe, ed., *The Green Studies Reader: From Romanticism to Ecocriticism* (London and New York: Routledge, 2000).
  This collection of extracts on ecology, eco-literary criticism, and eco-philosophy makes a good companion book to the Glotfelty and Fromm collection below. It includes Kate Soper's important discussion of the three understandings of "nature."

Cheryll Glotfelty and Harold Fromm, eds., *The Ecocriticism Reader: Landmarks in Literary Ecology* (Athens and London: The University of Georgia Press, 1996).
  This collection focuses on American ecocriticism, containing important essays by Lynn White Jr. on the Christian transcendence of modern science, Christopher Manes on animism and texts, Ursula K. Le Guin on the novel as carrier bag, Joseph W. Meeker on comedy as ecology, and more.

Val Plumwood, *Feminism and the Mastery of Nature* (London and New York: Routledge, 1993).
  A comprehensive and persuasive analysis of the philosophical and theological origins of the suppression of women and nature.

Kate Soper, *What is Nature? Culture, Politics and the Non-Human* (Oxford and Cambridge: Blackwell, 1995).
  A scholarly yet accessible analysis of the heritage of and philosophical issues around terms such as "nature" and "culture."

Jung the Writer on Psychotherapy and Culture

[W]hen Jung was with Antonio Mirabal [Mountain Lake], he had "the extraordinary sensation that [he] was talking to an Egyptian priest of the fifteenth century before Christ."[1]

Cultural Difference: Two Trips to America (1909/1925)

Jung made two trips to America, both of which were to have an important effect on his life and work. In 1909 he travelled with Sigmund Freud, and in 1925 he went as an independent psychologist. The journeys proved to be profound encounters with culture and difference.

Witnessing the diversity of America brought together a series of important issues for Jung. These included: how to make a psychological theory; the role of the personal and subjective in relation to the collective; and the history of traditional healing versus the recent development of psychoanalysis. He was also struck by the gulf between cultures and its consequences for the imagination. He wondered how belief in science could relate to belief in God. Lastly, he felt provoked to consider the weakness of Western modernity, particularly as manifested in the horrors of the First World War.

Bringing together all these issues was the problem of pinning down the psyche in writing. How is it possible to communicate, in sensible words, the fluidity, texture, and fantasy-fuelled nature of the mind? Moreover, how is it possible to write authentically of the psyche in ways that could contribute to its healing? What is the most effective form for words of psyche, i.e., psychology?

All these questions became the heart of a book that Jung published in English in 1933, *Modern Man in Search of a Soul.*[2] Its title expresses the breadth of Jung's vision. Not just patients, not just those able to pay for analysis, but the whole of modern culture itself was his concern. Much of this chapter will look at two of the essays from this book, "Basic Postulates of Analytical Psychology" and "The Spiritual Problem of Modern Man." We will follow Jung's quest to find a form of writing that might address the wider culture. By examining the structure of these essays, we can see how the reader is drawn into a web of meaning designed to explore and reform (re-form) the modern psyche.

First of all, the differences in Jung's two trips to America are instructive in revealing the cultural problems that his writing begins to tackle. In 1909, Jung accompanied Freud as the junior partner when both were invited to lecture at Clark University. Tales emerge from this trip of the growing tensions between the two men. It was here that Jung realized that their theoretical differences could no longer be masked. The pivotal occasion was, appropriately, the discussion of a dream.

Walking with Freud in New York's Central Park, Jung described a dream: he is in the upper storey of an old house filled with Baroque and Renaissance furniture, and as he descends to a lower level, he finds a medieval floor. Lower still, there is a Roman basement. Finally, Jung finds a trap door in the floor and goes even further down, into a cave with human skulls.[3]

Freud's reading of the dream concentrated on the skulls. Sensing his anxiety about a death wish, Jung said that these belonged to his wife and sister-in-law. Freud was relieved, but Jung remained unsatisfied by the diagnosis. Rather, he felt that the dream was the expression of a deep mystery; it pointed to a historical quality in the unconscious. Later he was to call this quality the collective unconscious.

The 1909 trip to America was an attempt to repeat European colonialism in a supposedly "untamed" territory. This party of psychoanalysts saw themselves as bringing potent European practices to the ignorant New World. Legend has it that Freud and Jung stood together as their ship entered New York harbor, with Freud saying: "If they only knew what we are bringing to them."[4] He was worried about the reaction to his insistence on the sexual underpinnings of his psychoanalysis. In fact, this collision of European and American culture proved to be less stormy than the differences that the psychoanalysts brought with them.

Years later, in 1925, Jung had completed the task of working through his theoretical debates with Freud and was now independent. Instead of travelling to bring European sophistication to raw Americans, his main object was to seek out and experience cultural differences for himself. He especially wanted to meet Native Americans.

This time Jung had intermediaries for his encounter with the native people of the Taos Pueblo.[5] Jaime de Angulo was Spanish and worked closely with Native Americans; his first wife was Dr. Cary Fink, who had worked with Jung and later married his associate, Peter Baynes. As Cary F. Baynes, she with W.S. Dell did the English translation of *Modern Man in Search of a Soul*. Cary Baynes, through de Angulo, introduced Jung to a Pueblo elder, Antonio Mirabal, or Mountain Lake, as Jung was to style him.

Jung found Mirabal extraordinarily impressive, drawing the analogy with the Ancient Egyptian priest at the head of this chapter. In fact, Mirabal's discussions seem to have stuck to two subjects: in the first place, that white Americans should stop interfering with tribal ceremonies or the sun will not rise in ten years; and secondly, accusing these same Americans of being crazy because they think with the head and not with the heart.[6]

Mirabal wrote to Jung in 1932 to emphasize that he had not betrayed any tribal secrets.[7] But even if Mirabal had divulged little, Jung had intuited much. Just as the dream recounted to Freud in 1909 remained very significant to Jung, quite apart from the theoretical or personal conflict, so from Mirabel, the cultural Other, Jung acquired a powerful image of Western imperialism. This image became for Jung a symbol (see Chapter 3 on images and symbols) with a lasting effect on his writing.

Jung records in *Modern Man in Search of a Soul* hearing Mountain Lake talk about the white men, and a cruel figure comes into his mind: "the Aryan bird of prey with his insatiable lust to lord it in every land …"[8] Here is a clear example of Jung's encounter with another culture becoming the stimulus of *his own* creative imagination. Moreover, the fierce Aryan bird is not a neutral or merely descriptive image; it is politically and morally charged. From meeting Mountain Lake, Jung gains a *post-colonial* vision. He sees his own imperial culture, momentarily, with the eyes of an-Other, one grievously wounded by it. So here, in the cultural symbol generated by encountering a man from another culture, is a charged fragment of political vision.

Writing and the Psyche

What Jung discovered in America in 1925 is that cultural difference challenges us much as the unconscious does. Both undermine our sense of self-possession, our sense of securely knowing ourselves in the world. As Jung perceptively recognized, cultural difference is one important way that the unconscious takes hold of us. The rich complexity of what we do not know becomes the foreign language of our own psyche. Indeed, the metaphor of entering an unknown wilderness is one he uses.

> The moment one forms an idea of a thing ... [o]ne has taken possession of it, and it has become an inalienable piece of property, like a slain creature of the wild that can no longer run away ... [9]

He also says, however, that if we believe we completely comprehend some aspect of the psyche, then it is not true understanding; instead, it is the kind of science that knows wildlife by killing and dissecting it. For the psyche is a true wilderness of nature, where the domesticated ego is out of its natural habitat. We must learn by observation and with respect for the mysteries of all that is Other than the knowable part of ourselves, the ego.

This is a fascinating ecology of writing and suggests how much Jung became a kind of organic gardener of the psyche. The Jungian psyche is alive and populated in a way that is independent of the ego. So writing needs to invoke the voices of the Other and not repress them, not turn them into "slain creatures". Although Jung uses concepts and rational language in his psychology, his psyche-logos, he insists that such schematic language leads away from the living mystery of the creative unconscious. [10] Other more evocative, artistic, metaphorical, and even playful kinds of language are needed to let the psyche breathe in writing.

In *Modern Man in Search of a Soul*, Jung demonstrates how metaphor can evoke what can never be fully contained in writing: the protean essence of unconscious creativity. So, for example, Jung will personify the collective unconscious as a two-million-year-old man. Such a powerful metaphor is immediately followed by an alternative: that the unconscious is more like a constant stream of images.[11] Elsewhere he calls drama and myth "more expressive" and also "more exact" than abstract scientific terminology.[12]

Just as Jung aimed at wholeness in his treatment of patients, so too did he invite wholeness of psyche into his writing. The result: fascinating multi-voiced texts that re-orient the boundaries between science and art. Jung is acutely aware that in writing, as in psychology, there is no simple separation between the observer and the observed, author and matter. His powerful portrayal of the theoretical psychologist as "Big Game Hunter" shows one who slaughters what he claims to study. Such insight demonstrates sensitivity to cultural and colonial mind-sets that are capable of contaminating the practice of psychology as well as its writing.

He is saying that theory which purports to know all is as lethal to the living psyche as the colonial hunter to the native life of the wilderness. Implicitly, this calls for a post-colonial approach to the indigenous population of the psyche. It suggests that Western modernity's political dominance of the Other (as colonized subjects) has had fatal consequences for the inner Other (as unconscious potential).

Jung found, in his encounters with American cultural difference, a point of view that could reflect back the deficiencies of his European heritage. His "house of history" dream and the Aryan bird of prey symbol were his inspirations to seek out inner colonies, and he came to look upon the inner landscape with a new respect for its native vitality.

Coming from an intellectual culture built upon the supreme value of reason, on the suppression of all that is irrational and unconscious, Jung feared that Enlightenment values had ripped through the psyche like a Big Game Hunter, stripping unknown lands of native life. Too many of his patients felt dead inside—how could it be possible to revive the modern soul? For now it lies corpse-like under an ego grown inflated and dangerous. Indeed the very integrity of the ego is imperiled because its capacity for reason has been privileged to an unreasonable degree.

Writing and Culture: The Spiral Essay Form

The Wounded Researcher[13] is an important book by Robert Romanyshyn, further developing Jung's realization that modernity needs to invite psyche or soul into the heart of its learning (see also Chapter 7). No longer can we afford to cut our psyche in two, forcing rationality into one part and compelling the Other to take on the role of Other as irrationality, love, mystery, darkness, and the sacred. The dangerous state of the world requires the resources of the whole psyche, not a psyche crippled by division.

Romanyshyn suggests bringing the creative unconscious into learning through an alchemical, hermeneutical spiral of interpretation. Individuation energies of many kinds are drawn into the reading of a text regarded as symbolic, i.e., as pointing to what is not yet known or knowable.[14] The whole psyche, the whole soul, can fully participate in the research. Romanyshyn is arguing for "spiral reading," where hermeneutics or the art of interpretation winds around the text. This important idea inspires my suggestion that many of Jung's shorter essays, especially those in *Modern Man in Search of a Soul*, are spiral *in form*. I am suggesting that Jung wrote like this as a way of incorporating more of the psyche.

Jung's spiral essays wind around their themes, going deeper and wider into historical origins and cultural analogies. The reader is given a *process* captured in ideas and images, more than a definitive statement or conceptual argument. Put another way, the spiral essay works more through the rhetorical arts of persuasion by analogy and metaphor than through the logical methods of amassing evidence to "prove" a thesis.

Moreover the spiral essay form works to emphasize the *gap*, the hole in the middle. Through its twisting and pivoting work, the "hole" or absence of meaning in the essay is reconfigured as the "whole" by the spiraling of the essay itself as a symbol. The spiral essay form symbolizes the fullness of psyche, based upon an acknowledgment of the inexpressible, of that which cannot be fully known. The spiral essay is a form that enacts its matter: the centering of the psyche on mystery. It acts out the decentering of the ego and its form of rational, conceptual argument.

In these essays on culture, Jung wants to shift from an ethos of rational transcendence to one of immanence. From transcendence to immanence means from rational, so-called universal concepts to ideas embedded in a particular time and place. In a Western world taught to revere reason, truth, and concepts as transcending the matter they purport to describe, Jung wants to reconnect reason to the rest of the psyche. He aims to return reason and truth to a living connection with the true nature of the psyche in creativity.[15] He suggestively speaks of reconnecting rationality to the unconscious as "mother" in the maternal nurturing principle of fantasy.[16]

One way of understanding this far-reaching reorientation of the modern world is in the terms of mythos and logos as described in Chapter 1. Here I want to emphasize that mythos stands for myth or narrative as the fundamental element of knowledge or culture. Its alternative is logos, which means abstract knowledge *derived* from mythos. The ancient Greeks began this privileging of logos over mythos, a process that accelerated in modernity when scientific concepts were given supremacy over narratives such as those of religion (see also Chapters 4 and 5).[17]

Jung's de-centering of rational logos knowledge and his embrace of a psyche of many stories shows him trying to restore mythos to the parched landscape of the modern world. Indeed, in the spiral essays, Jung's creative *psyche-writing* situates Jungian psychology as a myth for modernity because it presents itself as rooted in a particular person and culture, as *one possible* narrative and not as an over-arching grand theory that purports to explain all, to possess and control all meaning. To the psyche, Jung says, a grand theory is a big gun, not a figure it can talk to.

Whereas grand theory claims the abstract truth of logos as *transcendent* over historical cultures of knowledge, Jung's psyche-writing as mythos, with its stress on a historical continuity of ideas, is immanent. Jung says his psychology is a historical development from previous related ideas. It is an individual myth because it is located in time and place; yet it is also another manifestation of a long history of psychic expressions. One structural form for this, which proves integral to Jung's vision of culture, is the intimate and cosmic relation between space and time.

Jung explores cultural difference by framing a meaningful connection between space and time. Such a strategy has flaws, in particular his identification of culture far away in space as being distant also in time, i.e., unsophisticated, compared to his own. Jung in this way slips into colonial language, calling tribal cultures "primitive" and likening them to the people of Europe's distant past. Yet aside from lapsing into his culture's lazy prejudices, his deeply intuited sense of cultural space through ideas of historical time proves to be a fascinating form for the imagination.

After all, Jung's aim in these essays is to move, or rather to literally *dis-place*, the European narrative of intellectual and cultural superiority. Jung seeks "Other" ground for the modern psyche than its smug satisfaction with its supposedly rational ego. So the landscape of a foreign culture becomes an invaluable vantage point from which to view Western modernity. From the point of view of the Other as other culture, it is possible to penetrate the Western world's assumption of its own benign rationality. It is then possible to discover its ruthless nature: the Aryan bird of prey.

To sum up: spiral essays de-center modernity's claim to moral and epistemological superiority. In the space left by the dethroned Western imperialist ego, the symbol of the bird of prey offers knowledge through the imagination and the heart. Spiral essays manifest the unknown psyche at the center; they realize it, show it to be real. The unconscious is revealed as a source of previously unknown in-sight yet always remains mysterious, partially unknowable. In this style of writing, it is the creative psyche that orients the reader, not the rational ego's logic. Jung's essay, "The Basic Postulates of Analytical Psychology," for example, challenges reason and abstract theory, while "The Spiritual Problem of Modern Man" contests the supremacy of Western values.

"The Basic Postulates of Analytical Psychology"[18]

Jung offers an epic historical narrative in order to frame and ground the ideas behind his proposed form of psychoanalysis, which he called analytical psychology.

Greece, Rome, and the European Middle Ages are all examples of historical cultures that believed in the independent reality of psyche or soul, while today's scientific materialism regards psyche as derivative of bodily matter. Such a revolution in consciousness also has a spatial dimension that is reflected in cultural practices. Pre-Reformation Europeans were nurtured in a consciousness molded by the symbolism of the Catholic Church. As incarnated in their great cathedrals, they saw themselves in a vertical relationship looking "up" to God. Once rigidly hierarchical Catholicism broke up, Europe started to look outwards in voyages of colonial expansion. These were accompanied by a parallel psychic movement: an exploration of physical matter in empirical science. Thus does Jung argue for the historical structuring of the psyche.

He suggests that the European psyche after 1600 became re-aligned as spatial and horizontal rather than vertical and temporal. The psyche manifested itself in the ego through the notion of space, acted out culturally through the colonizing of "Other" lands. In keeping with this colonial mastery of space in the new formation of the ego was the development of a science that downplayed spirituality. Eventually, physical matter seemed to be the only answer to all sensible questions of origin.

Jung introduces modernity from the point of view of an Other: the religious world view it replaced. By establishing two pivots—of *time*, in the beliefs of the past; and of *space*, in two different types of consciousness—he sets up a framework to undermine modernity's secure sense of its own foundations. In particular, the similarities he finds between prior vertical beliefs in spirit and contemporary horizontal matter prepare the reader for an astounding claim. The psychic revolution from vertical spirit and time to horizontal space and matter is more apparent than real, for today, matter is the "creative god" of our modern world![19] As Jung shows, for today's world, matter is presumed to explain the presence of everything; matter is thus being treated as the divine principle. The only difference seems to be the lack of a godhead's traditional qualities of personality.

Jung takes the evidence of the historical past and of the materialist present and makes of them a spiral that suggests the unknown. We do not know whether it is god or matter who governs our being. Neither can be proven to be the root of being; we merely discover that different historical periods have preferred one explanation or the other. Yet this very desire for an underlying explanation itself exemplifies a continuity rather than a dramatic break with the past. Hence styles of consciousness, seemingly native to the past, can spiral into the present and not be entirely dismissed or *out of place*.

If matter is god as the whole truth of things, then the psyche is a merely the product of our glands. This offers us a psychology without psyche, as Jung says in a superb rhetorical flourish. A psychology *with* the psyche means one asserting an autonomous psychic existence. To simultaneously discover and create such a psychology, one must go back to the spiritual past or look away from modernity to non-Western societies. For so-called "primitive" man, the psyche is a real presence with whom he converses.[20] Here Jung refers to his example of the Pueblo Indians telling him that true thinking is done with the heart.

Almost exactly at the center of "The Basic Postulates of Analytical Psychology" one finds the beautiful image that imaginatively frames the entire essay: the psyche is either mathematical point or universe of stars.[21] Again the writing pivots, from abstract point to grand cosmos. Jung uses the pivot rhetorically to free up the question of the psyche from fixed presuppositions. Metaphor and pivot clear a space at the center for image and imagination. Is the psyche an abstract equation in the human self, or an essence of life that is truly cosmic in dimension?

Rhetorical questions are also useful for dis-placing reason and linear argument. If the psyche is autonomous and non-corporeal then how can it disappear? No wonder the non-Westerner regards it as divine. Jung then swiftly switches to argue from biology by appealing to the instincts of animals: they seem to have an inborn source of knowledge that is replicated in behavior, so why should not humans similarly inherit patterns for operating our lives? Indeed, if we have an unconscious with inherited potentials, then we could characterize the soul metaphorically as either a two-million-year-old man or as an unceasing stream of images. Thus does imaginative writing evoke, cajole, woo, yet never definitively capture the essence of the unconscious.

Such an approach makes definitive philosophical statements impossible. Some may call God energy or effectively be treating energy as a god. All we can say with confidence is that these are words for something real, although Jung insists that the nature of that reality can never be finally known. Then he pivots again to the subject of knowledge as *affected* by that unknown reality. Whatever psyche is, it surrounds us and conditions all experience. Psychic reality is real because it is immediate experience, even when it transforms and misrepresents another reality to us.[22]

Primitive man respects psychic reality in that, for him, the gods still walk on earth. Conversely, modernity has replaced respect for the psyche with trust in reason, which failed utterly to save us from world war.[23] By contrast, Jung believes that religion is psychologically healthy when it provides genuine connections to the unconscious within and without.[24] Many patients suffer from a loss of meaning in their lives. Without spiritual principles to orient them to the unknown psyche, to the awe and joy of the creative soul, they become neurotic.[25] Western modernity is sick because it has lost authentic psychic spirituality.

However, it would not be true to the spiral to end on a blanket condemnation of Western materialism. Jung returns to questions of history and non-Western peoples on the way to an open ending. Psychology is compared to medicine at the time of the great switch in consciousness from horizontal to vertical. Such cultural practices as tribal initiation rites and Hindu yoga exist today even though they are not understood. Finally, the psyche remains a "riddle."[26]

"Basic Postulates" is an essay of ambitious pivots, provocative claims, evocative metaphors, and startling images. Its rhetorical aim is to decenter reason and rational argument. It wants to establish imagination, feeling, metaphor, and human history as equally valid modes of knowledge of the psyche. The spiral form of "Basic Postulates" enacts its argument that the unknown psyche, those mysteries signaled by the "collective unconscious," should be the center of modern life and its writing.

"The Spiritual Problem of Modern Man"[27]

There is a trickiness at the opening of this fascinating look at the delusions of Western modernity. Here, by "modern man" Jung means the individuated being. This modern man's happy psychic state is pictured spatially as him standing upon a mountain top. He has the history of mankind below, the future straight ahead, and the numinous cosmos above him. "He" has transcended the past rather than ignored it; but because he is not imprisoned in the conventions he was born into, he may appear untraditional.[28]

What a contrast to those who are not *modern*, in this essay's sense, but who merely *live in* modernity! These hopeless persons are "uprooted" by modernity's rejection of the religious past. Fated to be estranged from the true psyche, they are "bloodsucking ghosts" and "worthless."[29] Unaware moderns live unconsciously, like primitives, Jung says (betraying, however, his own intuition about space and time by mixing it up with a social hierarchy marked by the prejudices of his era).

People living unconsciously in modernity are not modern to Jung because he defines the modern age as the result of a historical progression of increasing consciousness. To be truly modern is to be individuated, including having a psychic sense of the past (see Chapter 4). The essence of his preferred modernity is the immanence of immersion in history, combined healthily with individuation's transcendence into a consciousness still aware of its roots in the past. Such authentic consciousness of the truly modern man relies upon a living connection to the unknown psyche. A crucial way of intuiting the unknown is to develop a profound sense of past culture.

Since Jung believed non-Western peoples to have different consciousnesses, he tended to lapse into the colonial way of regarding them as *behind* modernity. The analogy of so-called "primitives" and the unindividuated in his own society is Jung at his most reactionary. On the other hand, it does point to an interesting structure in his picture of society: a depiction of culture as containing different layers of psychic history.

The essay returns to modern man, who may now appear old fashioned in his reverence for past styles of consciousness. It is this very "backward looking" that releases him from social conformity: he no longer has to define himself against contemporary conventions. In addition, modern man must guard against falling into the Enlightenment illusion that modern consciousness represents the summit of human perfectibility.[30]

After all, two thousand years of Christian teaching has not created paradise. We are instead in an age of world war, barbed wire, and poison gas. Jung condemns in the most explicit terms the failure of Enlightenment ideas to bring peace. (Jung, in a rhetorical strategy of denial, won't claim that the white races are diseased, *but* ...[31]) Western modernity does not have the cultural and spiritual resources to restrict violence. The truly modern man, says Jung, writing between world wars, is he who knows as much.

Having established that the present is a culture of world war, Jung's project of de-centering Western values now proceeds to invoke the mysteries of space and time by comparing and contrasting non-Western *cultural space* and *historical time*.

In past times and other cultures, ancient Egypt for example, the psyche was "outside" and not imagined as contained within the body. A huge historical and spatial shift occurs when the discipline of psychology is founded. Such a revolution was necessary, Jung believed, because the rituals of Christianity were no longer capable of regulating psychic energy.

Also, at this historical moment of the founding of psychology, war was no longer just a matter of "outside." After the total devastation of World War I, bitter conflict had penetrated within. Does the creation of psychology as a language of the "inside" contribute to the inner migration of war? Jung is not explicit about this, yet encourages speculation. Moreover, by saying that we are "at war with ourselves," Jung is starting to deconstruct the boundaries between outer and inner that modernity has erected.[32] War in this new world threatens to explode the psychic borders that psychology so carefully established.

For no longer can we simply regard all that is "foreign" to be our enemy. To be truly modern, man must realize ("make real") that the enemy is inside himself and interior to his collective world. Modernity differs from previous cultures because it has no exterior institutions capable of regulating our dark impulses. We must grapple with the oppositions within, lest we fatally repeat our society's mass delusions of the enemy outside us.

To dramatically represent modernity's peril, Jung contrasts the psychic universe of medieval man to today. Then, all were children of God. Now we are traumatically split between Enlightenment humane values and the feeling that we have to defend them with poison gas.[33] Here in Jung's writing, the dark inner Other becomes the "devil" who will be unable to prevent himself from unleashing weapons of mass destruction. Naming this powerful force as "devil" links deracinated modern man with the psychic universe of the medieval "child of God." Writing connects one psychic age to another, just as Jung asks us all to do. It *is* possible for split modern man to grasp a more authentic existence. There is a way to psychic wholeness through evoking the past.

Nevertheless, the essay tells us that there is more work to do before the modern soul can forge a link between psychic space and historical time. For now, Jung wants to emphasize the suffering of the modern person. Inner life is no refuge from a violent world; it is itself the home of chaos.

The world's terrors have moved in. In a rhetorical overcoming of the subject/object division, we have the example of a politician whose erratic behavior ought to provoke a mass outcry that he be analyzed at once! As Jung concedes, this does not happen. It is a serious mistake to believe that what is psychic is under our control.

Yet all is not lost, for there are psychic resources to be found in our culture, even if on the margins. These do promote a healthy integration of psychic energy. The arts are an example of ancient ways of shaping the soul that continue to evolve in modern times (see Chapter 3). So powerful is the potential of art that it is sometimes prophetic of the future collective psyche, as well as being rooted in historical depths. The true artist, in any age, reaches deep into the collective unconscious.

Of course, Jung preferred religion as a mediation between the individual ego and the wilderness of the psyche. Since modern man has lost the immanent connection with mainstream religion, Jung turns to the religious margins. What values have the esoteric practices developed, he wonders, in order to rebuild a psyche-infused spiritual symbolism? Such activities as astrology, spiritualism, and theosophy are creative attempts to recall the spiritual mind-set of the past. They resemble Gnosticism, of which Jung approves, regarding it as able to encompass the whole psyche, including the shadow. With gnosis signifying knowledge, Jung sees today's psychic attitude as gnostic for its pursuit of religious experience over doctrine. Modern man wants to discover the *reality* of the psyche through spiritualism, theosophy, etc. "Psychoanalysis" may be, in essence, another such neo-Gnostic system for feeding this appetite for inner reality.

Jung's cultural theory is a story of self-regulating social entities, themselves possessing an individuating drive to wholeness. He sticks to a level of generalization in his account of culture that risks glossing over specific and localized material. However, his holistic vision of how cultural structures incarnate psychic creativity has intrinsic and enduring value. While this notion is inherently conservative, suggesting a fundamental stability that could lapse into stagnation, what saves it is the core role of the Other. As always, the Other as unconscious can be embodied in the arts, culture, religion, the past, the future, or a different culture. Jung's cultural theory draws into the collective psyche those who are fundamentally

different (medieval man, Indians) as necessary aspects of psychic wholeness. Indeed, Jung's cultural theory is a revolutionary conservatism that
largely respects the Other by not ever claiming to entirely know or fully
appropriate it.

His vision of the psyche and culture is one of "nested" wholes: we have
an individual being who is contained in various cultural practices, in the
nation and maybe other collectives like the modern West, in humanity,
and finally in the cosmos.[34] So we are all both separate unique selves and
one, a whole individuating being.[35]

Modern man may have lost the psychic attachment to religion, but
the psyche is still alive and pinned to "Other" gods. The gods we need
to dethrone now are the Western values that prevent us from truly individuating. By invoking the past and other cultures, we might be able
to mitigate the real blackness of our souls. Anything that we hold as
unchallengeable truth, be it Freudian psychology or the ideas behind the
Russian Revolution, is a god made blind by its very unchallengeability.

Blind gods are really our own blindness, our illusions about the beauty
of the Western soul. In a striking image, Jung writes that we Westerners
treat ourselves as idols. Cultural arrogance makes us burn incense to
ourselves and so mask our eyes with smoke.[36] We ourselves create the
obscuring mists that prevent us from seeing what we truly are. Only the
eyes of the Other can save us in such a tragic situation.

The cultural Other is particularized with the introduction of Antonio
Mirabal, who appears in Jung's work as Mountain Lake. Mirabal speaks
of his people's bewilderment at the crazy attitude of the whites. In doing
so, he paints a portrait of the white-skinned mask as one of cruel, sharp
lines. Now, with the contribution of this Other, Jung generates his own
image of the underside of his political culture. White modernity is "the
Aryan bird of prey with his insatiable lust to lord it in every land."[37]

We see here the *process* of this essay embodied in its *matter*. Jung down-
plays rational analysis about the character of European civilization in
favor of argument using imagination; he allows contact with the Other
to stimulate images. His method of argument draws images bearing fragments of (Other) consciousness from culture, history, rhetoric, ritual, the
esoteric, and emotion. His essay is one of many voices, and it is *about* the
necessity of hearing many voices of the psyche.

After such a passionate evocation of image as cultural criticism, the essay digs deep, deeper than any culture. It tells us that the psyche is, at root, nature, and that nature herself is creative life.[38] However much nature, as in the psyche itself, may be destructive, it is also the same nature that rebuilds. So we are reminded that nature is the larger framework of the psyche, framing the collective being of humanity. Jung implies that culture is housed in nature; culture does not oppose nature. This means that *psyche-logic*, the right healthy understanding of psyche, is also an *eco-logic*. The individual psyche is an organic expression of nature and will only thrive if understood as such. This vital re-writing of the de-spiriting of nature by modernity is very important for twenty-first century ecocriticism.

Entering the final phase of the essay, Jung circles back to pick up the topic of the Eastern Other in China, the Orient, and legends of theosophy. The essay is about to make a striking association of cultural space and psychic space. First of all, there is a simple pivot: Western materialism flows east yet at the same time Eastern spirituality overwhelms the West. Westerners conquer economically; Easterners triumph spiritually. As our neglected psyches become strange and even uncanny to us, so does the East become more hypnotically attractive, for it comes to signify our unknown selves.

It is not surprising that we find ourselves imitating the East in occult sects such as theosophy, or look to the sexual ideas of Hinduism. Our Western sense of superiority ought to be corrected by the discovery that new developments in science were anticipated in China. Such sophisticated advances by the Chinese include some of Jung's own psychology.[39]

Now the essay graphically realizes the obsession with the East. Theosophy tells a myth of holy men in an Eastern monastery manipulating every mind in the world. True to Jung's idea of myths, this contains a psychic truth, and he makes this mythological image into an important symbol. Our "Eastern directors" do lie within. The Western psyche, having lost touch with its deep energies, is attuned to an-Other power, an inner East (of archetypes).

Finally, the essay turns to the possible rooting of the psyche in the body. Jung notes approvingly the modern cult of the body in the growth of sport and dancing. Here is another way of denying a division between mind and matter. On the contrary, body and spirit are one: body is the material manifestation of spirit, while spirit is the living body from the psyche's point of view.[40] Today's attempt to strengthen the enfeebled consciousness of the West needs to engage with the instinctual body.

"The Spiritual Problem of Modern Man" ends by emphasizing the "hole" in knowledge of the psyche that is, at the same time, an evocation of the "whole." Jung's writing persona detaches himself from the essay as only one voice, one person's experience offering a "subjective confession."[41] His essay is a spiral that unravels Western superiority and provides the reader with striking material for the imagination.

Writing for Culture and the Alchemical Spiral

Notable in Jung's writings on psychotherapy and culture is his preference for enacting over telling. The writing *performs* his beliefs about the individuating soul. Creativity in his texts augments, it does not detract from, his formation of rational concepts. By their intelligibility and completeness, concepts are transcendent of argumentative *matter*. Yet while including such material, Jung makes the reader *experience the creative immanence* of the imagination as an essential component of a portrait of the *whole* psyche. By being a creative writer as well as a theoretical one, Jung is experimenting with fundamental epistemological notions of the relations between form and matter. This vital topic will be returned to, periodically, in this book.

Creative immanence in the writing takes two directions: one is the evocation of the "hole" in the spiral essay form that is the "whole" of the ineffable unconscious; the second direction is a dialogical response to culture. For Jung is clear that the psyche is a cultural organ, and that culture is the matter out of which we are made. Yet culture also does not *determine* who we are, for that would be to deny primacy to the creative psyche. Rather, culture is part of the earth in which we are rooted. It should nourish us and provide a route to the nature enclosing it.

Of course, a true psychic embedding in culture is, for Jung, also a historical sense of past styles of being. By an inner dialogue with what is familiar and what is strange in the past, we negotiate with our inner otherness as well. Similarly, true cultural *cultivation* must respect the difference of other cultures, and welcome their gifts to the imagination when they show us ourselves. Becoming who we truly are means becoming self-aware cultural beings. The collective outside us can unlock the mysteries of the collective unconscious inside us.

Such a principle allows us to recognize Jung's writing as a cultural and psychological *instrument*. By reading the spiral essays, the reader continually re-negotiates the meanings of outside and inside, the psychic and cultural imagination, while at the same time empowering the sense of dynamic mystery at the absent center. In this way, the spiral essays could be said to *individuate* the reader. All reading is a negotiation of meaning with a text. What marks out these spiral essays as different is that *this* negotiation de-centers the reader's sense of conventional beliefs (housed in the ego) and erodes the boundary between self and world, creating a liminal space. Jung's spiral essays individuate the reader by initiation into a social and historical world, on the one hand, and into the mysterious depths of the psyche, on the other.

Jung the writer is a culture *maker*. His writing as culture making is also writing as therapy. The individual psyche is nested in a particular society, in modernity (or against it), in humanity, and finally in a nature of cosmic proportions; the roots of our unconscious reach up to the stars. If the creativity of the spiral essays truly nurtures our vital connection to the unconscious, then it is an art that brings us home to nature.

For modernity is sick, according to Jung in 1933. Centuries of privileging rational knowledge have left us with nothing but conceptual "big guns" with which to approach the rest of the psyche, and too often such theoretical weapons devastate rather than rejuvenate the inner world. The horror of modernity is that the big gun of rational theory has become concretized in weapons of mass destruction because we do not know ourselves. Without genuine inner sympathy and self-awareness, we find ourselves overwhelmed by a dark Other exploding from within. Poison gas is a grotesque product from *within* Western modernity and from the dark unwitting souls of its inhabitants.

Jung often refers to himself as a scientist. He is, however, a scientist who insists upon artistic practices as central to both writing and therapy. While explaining that his work can never be pure art because it aims at exploring the unknown psyche and not at producing aesthetic value,

Jung is an unusual scientist in demanding priority for the creative unknown. Ultimately, Jung deconstructs the boundaries between science and art, revealing them to be *cultural*, and animated by assumptions that need re-examination. For these boundaries exemplify problematic divisions in modernity, such as between reason and feeling, that are creating the sickness of the modern world.

Jung's vision of mental creativity is of a wholeness that spans the parameters of science, philosophy, and the arts. These he wants to be attuned to reverence for the "hole" in the psyche where dreaming mysteries are born. With such tremendous ambition does he address an arid modernity longing for the rebirth of its creative being. While sticking to his assertion that he is no artist, Jung himself was drawn into the imaginative expressions of literature and painting. Later artists as well as psychologists found his work an inspiration for feeding the artistic soul. We will move on to the topic of Jung and the arts in Chapter 3.

FURTHER READING

Michael Vannoy Adams, *The Multicultural Imagination: "Race," Color and the Unconscious* (London and New York: Routledge, 1996).
  A groundbreaking book, highly recommended.

Paul Bishop, ed., *Jung in Contexts: A Reader* (London and New York: Routledge, 1999).
  A wide-ranging collection of essays exploring Jung's cultural, historical, and intellectual context.

James Hillman (Thomas Moore, ed.), *A Blue Fire: The Essential James Hillman* (London and New York: Routledge, 1989).
  James Hillman has taken Jungian ideas further and deeper than any other. This is a useful collection of pieces for those starting to explore his rich works.

Susan Rowland, *Jung as a Writer* (London and New York: Routledge, 2005).
  My book aims to open up the imaginative qualities of Jung's writing in order to look at the way it enacts as well as describes his ideas.

Jung for Literature, Art, and Film

Jung Meets James Joyce

When two great minds of the twentieth century first met, the encounter was not a success. In 1934, novelist James Joyce was in Zurich, where he had brought his mentally ill daughter, Lucia, for treatment.[1] Zurich was a particularly resonant place for Joyce, for it was in Zurich in 1915 that he wrote his great masterpiece, *Ulysses*, a novel set over the course of one day in the Dublin of 1904.[2] By a fascinating coincidence, at the very same time Joyce was writing *Ulysses*, Jung was in Zurich and undergoing extreme mental turmoil. Later he described this time of fears and visions as providing the insights for his entire career. In that small city, during the carnage of World War I, one man's descent into chaos existed beside another's triumphal formatting of the chaos of modern life into art. No wonder *Ulysses* later became significant for Jung.

The two men did not meet while Joyce was composing his novel. However, they were connected at that time by the same patron, a wealthy American, Edith McCormick. When Joyce seemed to be slow in completing his manuscript, McCormick suddenly ended her financial support. Joyce blamed the influence of Jung, who later admitted some responsibility. Jung had never advised McCormick on her relations with Joyce, he said, yet he had suggested ending a stipend to another artist who was failing to finish a project. Since the results of this treatment, throwing the artist on his own resources, were extremely productive, it is likely that Mrs. McCormick felt the method could be repeated.

So in 1934, it was only a sense of desperation that forced Joyce to ask Jung for a consultation. The disturbed Lucia has been placed in a private sanatorium, which Jung himself visited. Subsequently, she was extensively treated by Jung's friend and colleague, Cary Baynes. Due in part to the creativity of her female analyst, Lucia began to calm down. Unfortunately, her overall condition remained intransigent. Finally, in October, Joyce visited Jung to discuss his daughter's condition. Later reports suggest that they also discussed wider considerations of art and psychology.

As a professional consultation with a patient's family, it was not a satisfactory interview. Joyce had always refused to accept the seriousness of his daughter's condition, and Jung felt that he was not able to penetrate the layers of fantasy with which Joyce had surrounded his relationship with her. He said that he could not separate father from daughter because Lucia was her father's anima figure and *femme inspiratrice*, the feminine inspiration for his art. For Joyce to give up investing Lucia with his own deepest desires for creativity and libido would be to sever himself from his own unconscious.

From Jung's point of view, Lucia was paying the price of Joyce's genius. Perhaps, just perhaps, this insight was anticipated by the price he himself experienced when he read *Ulysses*. A few months after Jung and Joyce's conversation, Joyce removed Lucia and his family to Paris. There she deteriorated, and eventually she was permanently institutionalized.

Jung Meets a Work of Art: James Joyce's Novel *Ulysses*

Jung made an extensive critical analysis of only one work of art, James Joyce's novel, *Ulysses*. So while this chapter will consider what he said *about* the arts and how that has been *applied* to criticism of literature, the visual arts, and film (and television), it is worthwhile to begin with Jung as a practitioner of arts criticism.[3] And in connection with the sad story of Lucia Joyce, it is striking to note that his first reaction to *Ulysses* is that it made him ill!

Nothing happens in *Ulysses*. The single day in Dublin begins in a void and ends in one. Sentences go nowhere. Words and pages are a pitiless stream without meaning. Jung heroically manages to attain page one hundred and thirty five, falling asleep twice on the way. Yet he exclaims with increasing horror that the book is *seven hundred and thirty five pages long!* Monotonous and hypnotic, the novel paralyses the body by making it go to sleep.

At last an image arises for this monstrosity of a work: the tapeworm. To Jung, *Ulysses* is a cosmic tapeworm for it is endlessly capable of proliferating chapters. As a tapeworm *it inhabits the interior of his body and steals his nourishment*, his vitality. Reading is a process of ingesting a monster whose alien life force takes over one's own body and soul.

To read *Ulysses* is to be subjected to a horrific assault upon body and psyche. The book refuses to "mean," to be "digested" in the normal way. Jung is irritated with Joyce, blocked. The only way forward is to stop trying to read the novel and start trying to treat the distress of the reader. Jung, the therapist, has to resort to doing therapy on himself. The novel, in its tapeworm quality, is forcing him to have a conversation with his intestines!

Themes, Jung reflects, are the "scaffolding" for psychic events, including mental and physical paralysis.[4] As chains of meaning in a text, themes may be deliberately planted by the author or they may be consciously or unconsciously assembled by the reader. Can the tapeworm image constitute a theme? Jung certainly develops it here, as a way to imagine the de-souled, cold-blooded universe that Joyce depicts. Jung even turns to his professional background in wondering whether a diagnosis of schizophrenia applies to the book.

Fortunately, he conceded that the novel cannot be *solved* by removing it from art to pathology: diagnosis is no "solution." It is unable to dis-solve what is intractable in the novel. While describing a fragmented world moving in a ceaseless stream of sensation, the book is nevertheless written with careful selectivity.

Here Jung makes an important remark. *Ulysses* is not the uncontrolled product of mental illness, of schizophrenia. More subtly, the novel belongs to that sort of modern art which takes on some of the qualities of this disease to challenge and heal an alienated modern world. *Ulysses* is not the product of illness but rather a creative response to it. The novel is *about* cultural pathology. Whereas previously, an artist found a unity in his tortured personality by creating beauty and unity in art, today the modern artist finds his psychological *truth* in making art about the destruction of conventions and values.

Modern art, Jung realizes, is breaking up traditions of meaning and representation because they no longer work in the chaotic modern world. Indeed the terrible, meaning-resistant proliferation of the *Ulysses* chapters has a positive value in the very efficacy of its ruthless destruction! The visceral quality of *Ulysses*, with its emphasis on the workings of the physical body, reverses art: it is the "backside" of art![5]

In the relentless dirt and matter of the body there also emerges a historical dimension. *Ulysses* is Catholic art, harking back to the Middle Ages and the popular arts of the body. It evokes the stress which religious icons and practices place on bodily decay and death. Cold-blooded, visceral *Ulysses* arises to smash the sentimental forms that art and culture have since erected to save conscious life from its terrifying Otherness. Only by brutally sweeping away those sentimental structures can unconscious powers be liberated, and ultimately become less terrifying.

So the artist can be a prophet. He can through his art help to break through the surface sentimentality of the age, to compensate for the complacency and smug illusions of convention.[6] Fascinatingly, Jung follows this suggestion for the prophetic role of the artist with another, significant recognition that *Ulysses* resists interpretation. The work is not susceptible to straightforward decoding. It is not "symbolic" in the simplistic sense of being studded with instantly recognizable archetypal images that can be "translated" into the language of Jungian archetypes, which would, in any case, be to read "symbols" as *signs* (see Chapter 1 for Jungian notions of sign and symbol). This should be taken as a warning to future Jungian critics: a simple labeling of textual figures as anima, animus, shadow, etc., does not amount to *solving* the text.

Rather, Jung is going to find a *truly symbolic way of reading* Ulysses. His triumph will be to do so not by using a "theory" to strip away its recalcitrant aspects. Instead the novel, as instigator of chaos, *is itself* the source of in-sight by forcing the reader to change his or her perspective on society. So this particular interpretation is going to be concerned with the problem of wholeness, the problem of creativity in author and reader, and especially, with the problem of sickness—but here the sickness of the collective cultural consciousness. For it is Jung's own afflictions as reader, the inner-sight given by bodily and psychic assault by the "tapeworm" epic, that enables the novel as a whole to be as a *living symbol that creates a new consciousness for a new age.*

Back to the immense length of the book. Reading it is a multifaceted process; we look, as Jung puts it, at the world for seven hundred and thirty five days (those pages!) with the vision of the novel, with *Ulysses*. And in all that time, we do not find James Joyce the author. He is not there. His ego has dissolved into the many figures and events. *Ulysses*, the book, is the self. Crucially, *Ulysses* is the (Jungian) Self of Joyce, the artist. Yet, the novel is far more. *Ulysses*, the novel, is a Self *symbol* for the modern world. *Ulysses* is the wanderer seeking a home in the soul of the reader: *the novel seeks to guide the reader home.*

True, the novel makes the reader ill. Tackling that illness through continuing to do epic battle with the monster of the text, the reader and novel co-create a new consciousness. Together text and reader act out a detachment from the sentimentality of modernity. For Jung, this work of art profoundly re-organizes consciousness. It re-situates the myth of the wanderings of Odysseus, who becomes the reader adrift in the modern world. To read the novel is to navigate treacherous seas and frequently to get lost. In so doing, however, the reader has struggled with art as monster until the reader can "see" it as a way home. Jung has come to regard the novel as a possibility for re-making consciousness through the efforts of both body and psyche.

The "Ulysses" that Joyce's *Ulysses* presents is a textual being, a creature made in the reading process. "He" is comprised of characters but also of houses, events, streets, scraps of paper, etc. It is a perspective on modern life made *visionary* by its very challenge to conventional forms of meaning. Its focus on *things*, on the materialism of Western life, stimulates conscious realization in the reader. By the end of the novel, we come to a new consciousness of the misguided psychic investment we place in money and physical objects.

Indeed, what is perhaps especially provocative is the way Jung ultimately identifies the book with "whiteness,"[7] by which he seems to mean a quality in European culture that is sick due to its inability to appreciate the Other, including the racial Other. *Ulysses* is finally a spiritual work. The reader is made, by the sheer length and difficulties of the work, to take an epic journey into re-finding (which means re-forming) consciousness. He or she has struggled to find/form *home* as part of a collective struggle for a new consciousness for a new age.

Ulysses is symbolic if understood as a psychological tool for re-engineering the white Western soul with—and into—collective consciousness. If the reader cannot envision the book within his or her culture, then he or she is stuck battling a saurian tapeworm! It turns out that Jung has a lot to say about responding to art.

Against Interpretation and for Imagination: The Dangers of Interpreting Literature, Art, and Film

Jung is even more explicit about the perils of interpretation in an essay on poetry.[8] Here he says that psychology may not presume to "explain" (that is, to *explain away*) literature because there is no unifying principle in the psyche that would warrant it. Psychology, he believes, has not discovered a straightforward "truth" that would enable it to diagnose art or artists. Such a powerful break on the interpretation of art *through* Jungian ideas ought to be the founding principle of Jungian arts criticism.

Jung criticizes Freud for behaving as if the Oedipus complex were such a "unifying principle" in the creative mind. For Jung, the essential truth of the psyche is that there is no essential comprehensible truth. His "metaphysical" proposition is that the creative unconscious is the most fundamental thing about human beings. Since it is, at least in part, unknowable, there can be no one coherent, complete idea forming our minds, structuring our lives, or even generating our knowledge.

So if there is no unifying principle then there is no one type of knowledge, human activity, or academic discipline that can claim greater explanatory power than any other. In effect, psychology cannot be treated as more "true" than the arts. Therefore Jungian criticism, whatever it may be, cannot pretend to totally understand or explain works of art in any medium. Wholeness in the Jungian approach must include a sense of "holeness." An authentic Jungian arts criticism should leave a space for the unknowable Other in the work, in the audience, and in the artist. There will always be something *more* to be generated by the psyches of future critics and audiences.

Jungian arts criticism, we have learned so far, will be tentative about its own claims for understanding. It will respect the Other in all the materials including the psyche of the critic, and it will be aware of the symbolic mysteries inherent in the *collective* nature of works of art (see below). To a certain extent, then, we need to think of a Jungian approach to literature, art, and film as a practice *against interpretation, and for imagination.*

Jung's Four Interpretative Practices for Art, Literature, and Film

Jung is very open about the issue of language in psychology and how it might impact an approach to the arts. He points to psychology's use of the language of concepts and rational argument as offering an abstract categorization of experience. Such language, he tells us in the poetry essay, is necessary for intelligibility, yet is also profoundly inauthentic in representing psychic experience. Abstract concepts move away from the *feel* of the living mystery of the psyche.[9] So concepts about and classifications of the arts should be regarded more as principles, helpful to structuring an open investigation, rather than as absolute categories. While bearing this proviso in mind and further to the general psychology, Jung provides four starting principles for arts criticism.

In the first place, arts vary widely in the extent to which they invoke the whole psyche. The material of art, be it visual or written, is made up of *signs* and *symbols*. A sign is an image that principally stands for what is known and knowable. Take a Jane Austen novel such as *Mansfield Park*.[10] Here the title itself works as a sign for the great house around which the action of the novel revolves. But sign, in Jung's sense, means not just that the words identify a particular house, that these words as signifiers have particular meanings or signifieds. Rather, the title is the sign for this house as central to the conservative and knowable (the novel will teach us to know them) values of early nineteenth century British gentry.

The alternative to the sign is, of course, the symbol. Symbols point to what is relatively unknown, not yet known, or even unknowable. In the novel, *Wuthering Heights*, the moors on which the novel is set can be regarded as a Jungian symbol.[11] The moors seem to stand for a nature beyond human comprehension, without clear boundaries between life and death, a nature partaken of by the heroic and terrible pair, Catherine and Heathcliff.

Signs and symbols relate to notions of the conscious and unconscious psyche. This relation is not a simple binary opposition in which signs characterize consciousness and symbols the collective unconscious. After all, it is basic to Jung's psyche that consciousness is perpetually wooed, challenged, and enraptured by the unconscious in individuation. Consciousness is a *process* of creation *with* the unconscious. So signs belong *more* to consciousness, and make use of the collective consciousness (the agreed social system of conventional meanings) to affect us as social beings. Symbols have a *home* in the collective unconscious but are only *manifest* in consciousness.

However much symbols embody unconscious creativity, they must do so by using conscious materials or we could not even notice them. The moors of *Wuthering Heights* may reach deep into mysteries of sexuality, life, death, and the body, yet *in order to do so* they must capture the imagination by evoking something recognizable. The symbol needs representative material: descriptions of natural landscapes, cultural ideas, conventions about nature and self, and so on. No sign belongs purely to consciousness, or there would be no energy to its meaningfulness. No symbol is purely unconscious or there would be no possibility of meaning. It is by evoking an unspeakable and unrepresentable possibility of meaning that the reader/viewer is lured into the creative intensity of the art.

From signs and symbols, and with particular reference to literature, Jung felt that it was possible to classify written works into two categories. [12] *Psychological* literature is that in which psychic mysteries have been laid bare for the reader. It depicts a knowable social world. Hence psychological literature relies more upon signs than symbols. Jane Austen would be proud to be considered a "psychological" author. Conversely, *visionary* literature is mysterious to its own author, to itself, and to the reader. Such challenging work evokes the sublime and the daemonic, and rips away the thin membrane between chaos and reason. [13] By its very nature, visionary art is symbolic in Jung's sense.

As a way of categorizing literature, the division between "psychological" and "visionary" has value, but is in danger of becoming a rigid imposition of abstract ideas. It becomes something more when Jung concedes that these characterizations *may change over time*—a work may be regarded as visionary in one age and psychological in another, or vice versa.

This brings us to a third principle of art interpretation from Jung. Visionary art functions as a form of psychological compensation to the one-sided values of its culture. Just as the dream compensates for conventions and biases in the individual, visionary art, saturated with symbols energized by the collective unconscious, performs the same function for culture. If *Wuthering Heights* was a visionary work in 1847, then it surely compensated for Victorian sentimentality to do with sexuality and ideas of nature. Its evocation of storm and snow compensates a contemporary religion far removed from nature. Heathcliff's implacable ferocity may be a response to a culture that exalted reason at the expense of the Other. Arriving from an unknown origin and departing to an unknown destination, Heathcliff sows seeds of intolerable otherness across nineteenth-century England and, arguably, into the twenty-first century.

Indeed Heathcliff's potency brings us to the fourth Jungian interpretative principle for art: that visionary art may be best understood *teleologically*. Visionary art can show us where the culture is *going*. If we want to apply such a consideration to *Wuthering Heights*, then probably a twentieth century reading would note the depiction of sexuality as mysterious and unfathomable. Now in the twenty-first century, I might propose a reading that emphasizes the return of the repressed in the form of nature and the dispossessed.

Heathcliff is the ultimate outsider, whose mysteries touch upon both nature and culture. He brings the wilderness of the moors *indoors* to destroy a human society that cuts him off from what sustains his life (here Cathy, his beloved, works as a symbol). He is thus nature itself, dispossessed by Western modernity. Furthermore, he is also all those colonized peoples whose nature (in the sense of both psyche and land) has been polluted by Western culture. So he returns, vexing to destruction the fragile marriage of Cathy and the cultivated Edgar Linton—just as nature rises against us in global warming and the dispossessed peoples of the earth can no longer be kept from the door.

The combination of Jung's four principles of arts interpretation, together with concepts like archetypes and the Self, can be used effectively as long as the critic remembers two cautionary notes. Firstly, that for Jung the creative unconscious is the basis for all his ideas and therefore should infuse the critic as it does the artist. Secondly, all art, in any form, is cultural. It is not *determined* by culture because that would limit the role of the creative unconscious; for Jung, nothing can do that. However, just as all archetypal images are informed by a personal and cultural history, so is art. Remaining sensitive to cultural context prevents the conceptual side of Jung's ideas—concepts of anima, shadow, and so on—from severing the critic from the living mystery of the work as art.

A New Way of Reading?

In this section, I want to propose a modification to the use of Jung's psychological and visionary categories. Where he sees them as types of literary work, which may change according to the culture, I suggest regarding them as *types of reading*. It may help us to develop a creative critical practice (so being faithful to the creative unconscious) if we can focus on both the qualities of collective consciousness *and* of the collective unconscious in a work. Indeed, in the last fifty years, *Wuthering Heights* has been recognized as both psychological *and* visionary by literary critics without using these Jungian terms. Earlier criticism stressed the Romantic, sublime and thus visionary nature of the novel. More recently, research has uncovered the remarkable extent to which the novel incorporates contemporary social issues and religious disputes.

To test the psychological against the visionary as reading practices, what could be said about that devotee of reason and common sense, Jane Austen? I have argued that the title of *Mansfield Park* is a sign and that the work is largely psychological: Austen knows her characters and her world thoroughly, and the reader is given the impression of achieving the same. Yet surely much might be gained by reading the title also as a symbol.

It was the post-colonial critic Edward Saïd who began to open up what was literally unspeakable and actually unrepresentable about the house and its signification in *Mansfield Park*.[14] For the economy of Mansfield Park is built on slavery, and Sir Thomas Bertram, as a plantation owner who travels to Antigua in the course of the novel, is an owner of slaves. Of course, these economically crucial characters never appear in the novel and are never directly mentioned. Yet the novel is haunted by notions of transportation (of Fanny Price from the home of her birth to Mansfield), of servility and dependence, and of the way people are moved about for money. The novel treats these themes in the marriage plots, yet deeper resonances surely pervade.

No, slavery does not become a sign in *Mansfield Park*, for the anguish and suffering of the black slaves is nowhere knowable in the comfort of the great house. Yet just beyond the gates are the poor farm workers briefly glimpsed from a carriage. Once or twice the novel mentions servants whose exploitative working conditions also make the *signs* and *psychological* knowability of the upper class characters possible. Reading the novel as visionary, finding it also in possession of symbols of slavery and oppression, *allowing the Other to speak in the text*, brings in voices from *the unconscious of the novel itself*. If we always include the unconscious of the artwork, always also read the work as visionary, then we may find that Otherness to be social and collective, as well as personal and ecstatic.

Jung and the Arts: Theory and Practice

To read Jung's writing about art is to discover something important about his work as a whole. His writing is not an abstract, fully coherent, rationally organized collection of conceptual arguments. Rather, it is *grounded* in a particular place and time, and offers a *home* to the Other. It offers the Other a home in the forms of creativity, art, and indeed "Other" forms of knowledge. Consequently, Jungian approaches to the arts are both theory *and* practice. If the critic needs to find his or her creativity as the most fundamentally *Jungian* way of encountering art, then the roles of artist and critic become liminal to each other, in the sense that there are no fixed boundaries between them. Every critic must cultivate the artist within.

Jungian arts criticism will never be wholly transcendent of ("above" and separate from) the artwork. Jungian theory cannot pretend to abstract purity. Jungian arts criticism knows that in *framing* a work, making it in some way more open to the audience, it is both inside and immanent (connected) to the *matter* of the work as well as outside it and transcendent. Some element of abstraction, conceptuality, and rationality must be maintained for intelligibility, while immanent intimacy with the artwork seeks to touch and to convey some of its living mystery. Art, Jung suggests, is a material moment in which conscious and unconscious are in mutual embrace. The creation of the work is a moment recreated every time it is experienced, whether by reader, audience, or critic.

Jungian art criticism will be dialogical; it will depend upon a reciprocal movement between transcendent and immanent modes of the psyche, a dialogue between conscious and unconscious realization. Moreover, such arts criticism *will tell a story*, different every time due to its weaving of the contingent into meaning through reference to a scheme of ideas. The contingent is here the subjective and historical matter of the artwork (where it comes from in time, place, person), rendered aesthetic by the explosion of creative energy from the collective unconscious. Art is historical time infused with sublime creativity. It is a moment made material, in which matter becomes both immanent and transcendent.

As a result of these deep drives within Jung's writing, Jungian arts criticism is well placed to explore the issue of universals versus particulars. For such Jungian criticism resists the notion that any work of art can be purely universal, pure abstraction. After all, even paintings that consist of perfect, apparently abstract geometric shapes require recognition as art by reference to a specific *historical* tradition about art. Conversely, those critics and artists who want to keep art as close as possible to an individual moment, to something apparently uniquely personal or very specifically social, have to realize—to *make real*—something general enough in the work to render its very "individuality" noticeable to the public.

Jungian arts criticism is already structured according to a creative frame which sets up a dialogue between art as a form of universal truth and art as unique and personal. It already understands that human life and human creativity live in the tension between transcendent and immanent modes of consciousness. In this way, Jung situates art at the heart of the notion of creation itself. For Jung's own writing about the psyche, suspended between conceptual transcendence and immanent creativity, is an attempt to re-articulate the two great creation myths of the history of civilization, myths that underpin art and knowledge themselves. Indeed, Jung's relationship with creation myths will become an important theme for the rest of this book, for it grounds his attempts to address the pains and perils of the soul today.

Jung, Art, and Creation Myths:
Art Transforming Consciousness in History

Creation myths can be divided into two types, one privileging "Sky Father" and the other "Earth Mother."[15] Both signify structures of consciousness found in human personalities and cultures to varying degrees.

Jung's writing as a whole is an attempt to re-align the relationship between the two great creation myths that together—one dominant, one marginalized—have shaped today's world. Christianity most obviously prioritizes a version of the ancient Sky Father creation story: nature, earth, and matter are formed as separate from divine logos or the rational consciousness of a paternal deity.

Such a primal division has consequences for gender. Masculinity is elevated into patriarchy as transcendence. Maleness becomes associated with mind and rationality as separate from body, just as the Father God made material earth separate from "Him." In this scheme, one type of human being is associated with the divine, the other is Other, indeed. "She" is femininity thrust outside creative potency. She is "made," not "maker"—the feminine as nature, matter, and body.

Yet Sky Father myths do not reign alone; they replaced but did not eradicate the earlier story of the Earth Mother. "She" is the fertile earth as immanently sacred, meaning that the divine is within the earth, nature, and the body, not separated from them. The Earth Mother is nature as sacred, creative, and *generative in herself*. All humans are children of the Earth Mother without any gender hierarchy, for she is prior to the division into two genders. Earth Mother is consciousness as connection and feeling. She envisions humanity as defined through a *relationship to nature*, in which consciousness is devoted to an embodied existence realizing the spirit *in* matter, rather than transcendent of it.

Evidently, the two creation myths sponsor different types of consciousness. Post-Enlightenment modernity has privileged the transcendence of masculine reason at the expense of a connection to the Other (as unconsciousness, body, the feminine, etc.). It has therefore been one of the functions of the arts to preserve and foster connected "feminine" consciousness. Of course, Earth Mother consciousness is not restricted to the arts. Jung's own writing, as I have argued, is a dialogue of transcendent concepts (abstract and separable from the surrounding matter) and immanent matter (what is local, personal, resulting from other voices in the writing).

His writing attempts to reverse the divorce of rational language and immanent creativity in modernity's separation of science and the arts. Why does he want to do this? He wishes to forge a new relationship between the two types of creation myth, because when one becomes dominant for too long, consciousness itself weakens. Modernity's stress on reason is a development which derives directly from Christian insistence on transcendence and patriarchy. Privileging of Sky Father reason *over* its Other has starved humanity of the embodied creativity of the Earth Mother. What is most precious to Jung in a culture of polarizations is the creative and ultimately unknowable unconscious, concealed in the marginalized creation myth.

Jung thus deconstructs the cultural division between art and science. Much of what is described as "culture" stems from this division. He reveals what is at stake in separating off the arts from the sciences through his dialogical writing, which weaves the transcendent idea of archetypes with their immanent incarnation in historical reality.

The connection between history and myth will be developed in the next chapter. Here we should notice that art—as a creative dialogue between immanent involvement (in body, nature, unconsciousness, etc.) and conscious discrimination (which is transcendent of body, etc.)—*is also a vehicle for transforming historical consciousness.* Indeed, the dialogue between sign and symbol is ultimately a method of *in-corporating* the individual into his world.

Art incarnates psychic exchanges between the known world of collective culture and unknowable unconscious energies. So a work of art is a method of incorporating the individual in the collective *at both conscious and unconscious levels.* Put another way, art enables us to imaginatively explore our individual relationships with the two creation myths. As we unwittingly do so, we are becoming part of, yet not wholly absorbed into, our social world.

Moreover, if, as Jung says, signs and symbols, the psychological and the visionary, change over time, so that a work of art may be psychological in one age and visionary in another or vice versa, then Jung is suggesting that historical distance, the estranging passage of time, may become a vehicle for the Other. An Iron Age pot may, even in its regular beauty, not have qualified as art in its time. It was a pot for cooking, a materialized sign. Now, however, it is matter transfigured into mystery, of an age we can barely imagine. History itself becomes the *matter* of the imagination.

For the matter of art, its material immanence to its own time, is inspirited by Otherness. Art changes as cultures change, to enchant anew every spectator, reader, and witness. History is invigorated and materialized by art, and art likewise re-animates the creation myths in the audience. Crucially, however, while the creation myths of consciousness are not re-animated in later times exactly as they were for the artist, the difference in appreciating art over time is not absolute. As a dialogue of transcendence and immanence (pure ideas versus embodied matter), the artwork offers immanence in its origins as strangeness: its unknown origins preserve a *mystery* within its making. Yet the artwork itself is making connections across time: it offers a transcendence of its particularity and locality.

The viewer's psyche is able to create—from its immersion in its own immanent culture, and with a "hook" to transcendence offered by the distance and strangeness of the past as given form in the artwork—a consciousness that is newly creatively energized, as well as deeply historically founded. Art heals consciousness by re-aligning the two creation myths and reconnecting them to our collective reality, understood as present time psychically imbued with the past. In fact, to Jung, *art materializes the past into imagination*, which is to say, provides an embodiment of past consciousness that *spiritualizes* matter (see Chapter 5 on alchemy).

Film, Literature, and Art after Jung

Making

There is an obvious divide between artists who draw on Jung for artistic inspiration and in their creative practice, and Jungian clinicians who have developed art as therapy. The former *defines* him or herself as an artist, and is not aiming for greater psychic health; indeed, he or she is prepared to *suffer* for the sake of the work. In therapy, by contrast, there is a *healing focus* on the emotional pain and psychological turmoil of the maker of the artwork. Therapy also functions within a therapeutic and institutional framework, whereas the artist sequesters him- or herself away—figuratively, in the imaginary world of the art form, and often literally, by working in isolation. Art therapy is thus also intrinsically more collective, involving by necessity at least one other person, and sometimes more.

Poets and authors have testified to the impact of Jung's psychology in freeing the creative imagination. For example, Edmund Cusick writes of the enabling work of Jung on the anima, the feminine dimension of the male. For him, the notion of anima was peculiarly helpful in providing a framework of ideas by which to structure a poetry of desire.[16] Novelists as various as D.H. Lawrence, John Fowles, Margaret Atwood, Doris Lessing, Ursula K. Le Guin, Philip K. Dick, Saul Bellow, Lindsay Clarke, and Michele Roberts, to name but a few (see Further Reading at the end of this chapter), have integrated acknowledged Jungian themes into their work. Jung is also an overt influence on painters such as Jackson Pollock and filmmakers such as George Lucas (*Star Wars*) and John Boorman (*Excalibur* and *The Emerald Forest*).

However, the term "influence" does not really do justice to the dynamic effect of Jung's writing, with its structuring of relationships between abstraction and the contingent, and its embodiment of both immanence and transcendence. For example, Le Guin, Lessing, Dick, and Roberts have all used Jung to break down the limitations of the realist novel and to help liberate them from the constricting conventions of literary genres. They have sought forms in which to represent the Other as divine consciousness, as aliens, or as fantasy worlds, or to find new ways to re-present visionary politics. A particularly rich experiment is that of Lindsay Clarke, who transformed the epic poetry of Homer's *Iliad* and *Odyssey* into the novels *The War at Troy* and *The Return from Troy*.

The literary form of epic poetry tends to a privilege an aristocratic vision. It effectively has *one* voice, and communicates a singular and unified understanding of the world. By contrast, the novel, although it may contain epic-type heroes, always has multiple voices. Clarke builds upon the tension in Jung between oneness, as expressed in the notion of the governing Self (taking on the language of Sky Father transcendence), and many-ness, as expressed in the multiplicity of archetypes (a form of Earth

Mother immanence concerned with life as embodied and with the many voices of nature). Clarke weaves a coherent story (oneness) that neverthe-less tells of the evils and casualties of war (many-ness), an image of the Self's complex wholeness.

The novel as a form does not need a deliberate injection of Jung in order to become a container for many characters and points of view; it has always been this. At the same time, if a work of art aspires to (Jung-ian) wholeness, it must also be a container for a "hole," a gap in meaning and representation making space for the unconscious Other.

The Jungian Self is also a resonant image or symbol for the artist as a figure, and it does not require Jung's own linking of the Self with the god-image to see this figure as connected with the Father God myth. Indeed, some film critics, beginning with Don Fredericksen, have associated the notion of the "auteur director" with Self.[17] Because the auteur theory proposes that everything about a finished film can be attributed to the creativity of the director, the notion of the Jungian Self works effectively to include the collective dimension of filmmaking: the collective con-sciousness and unconscious are inflected through the archetypal images of the film. Additionally, of course, the "hole" in the film, its unknown mysteriousness, is a vital ingredient of both the film as art form and its auteur as Self symbol.

With those arts practitioners who consciously make use of Jung's ideas, making art is not wholly separate from theorizing about art. Develop-ments in poetry, film, literature and so on are simultaneously creative experiments that result in art works and in presentations of new theories of aesthetics. Also drawing these artists together is that their art-making takes place on the borderline between order and chaos. They make art in order to *re-make* consciousness, to invoke Earth Mother immanence in the desert of modernity where transcendence has become disconnected from her. Art here causes order and chaos to recognize something of themselves in each other; dualism becomes a marriage, not a war.

Reading, Witnessing, Experiencing (and Making Theories)

Many Jungian theories of art reception have been developed, from John Beebe's founding essay, "The Trickster in the Arts," to Don Fredericksen, John Izod, and Terrie Waddell on film, as well as Terence Dawson and

Susan Rowland on the novel. Important recent collections include *Post-Jungian Criticism*, edited by Baumlin, Baumlin and Jensen, and *Jung on Film*, edited by Christopher Hauke and Ian Alister.

These recent critics build on a history of Jungian criticism that employed archetypes as *structural categories* of artistic form. Earlier critics such as Annis Pratt and Bettina Knapp[18] treated Jung's writing as a source of conceptual ideas *only*, that is, as *a source of psychological authority* about literature and visual arts. This approach, however, misses what is *immanent* and *dialogical* in Jung's writing. While illuminating points might be made about erotic representation by employing Jungian archetypes like anima and animus, for example, such criticism risks being limited by Jung's own cultural prejudices. To take Jung as conceptual alone is to engage only with his transcendent mode. Without also his recognition of the conceptual in *dialogue* with embodied immanence, what could be regarded as the irrational voice of an-Other in the work becomes abstracted into his "theory" of the feminine, etc.

Moreover, Jungian structuralist criticism, in making art conform to concepts, actually strips it of what Jung knew to be art's unique value, its traversing of the borderline between chaos and order. The danger of Jungian structuralist criticism is that it domesticates art, making it fit for modernity's feeble consciousness. A more challenging approach, one that re-members the importance of the creative and partly unknowable unconscious, allows art to be re-animated by "the Other within the critic." It allows art to surprise.

The Jungian critics I have named above, from Beebe to Rowland, are unafraid of the mythical power Jung invokes in art's re-forming of consciousness. So they offer *Jungian art theory*, an approach that recognizes art's potential for providing psychological wholeness through the serious business of facing and working with the Other. Although individual critics differ in their unique inflections of the central relation between chaos and order (one critic, for example, may stress the capacity for wholeness, another, art's ability to render chaos bearable), Jungian art theory shares key themes. Among the intrinsic themes of Jungian art theory are the following: the liminal relation between theory and practice; the necessity of space for the Other; the paramount role of creativity in re-making consciousness; and art as both personal and collective experience.

John Beebe's essay, "The Trickster in the Arts," is an important break-through in exploring the aesthetic role of art in *provoking* dis-order and dis-ease in its audience. Focusing primarily on the example of *Hamlet,* Beebe explores the "demonic impact" of works that leave our minds at war,[19] that disturb our ability to make simple linear judgments. Beebe also builds on the notion of the Jungian auteur filmmaker by arguing that directors such as Hitchcock are engaging in a type of "active imagi-nation" when making films, meaning that they are being stimulated at least in part by unconscious images.

By "trickster," Beebe is referring not only to the art work but also to the artist, whose disruptive energy enables art to break out of old pat-terns. Indeed, such "trickster-art" breaks out of the formal frame of the work and *in-corporates* the audience's disturbance as *part of the art.*

Returning to *Hamlet,* Beebe finds the work acting as the audience's progressive initiation into psyche's trickster figure. For the trickster pre-vents us from being swallowed up by a dark Other. The trickster drags audience members into experiencing their own capacity to do evil, and in this way, the trickster-art/artist fulfills its archetypal role of keeping our human potential for evil in front of consciousness. Beebe shows that much art is intrinsically trickster-like: it is a social entity that nevertheless delights in overturning conventional expectations. The trickster is art as chaos, and yet as the only defense against chaos.

Beebe ends by discussing how the trickster, once integrated (through the painful experience of "his" art), can contribute to other forms of psy-chological development. He can, for example, participate in the work with the anima. In da Vinci's *Mona Lisa,* trickster and anima are allied, and the creative mysteries spin on.

Of course, no art is, in Jungian terms, "pure" trickster, unless the trickster is taken to signify all types of plurality and otherness. We must remember that no archetypal representation *is pure,* for archetypes are mere hypothetical unions of transcendent abstract and immanent cul-tural realizations. For art to be art it must, in Jungian terms, be home for the Other. Terrie Waddell, like Beebe, notes that our culture needs to develop the trickster aspect of art. She concentrates on how certain films and television series help resolve cultural and psychological ten-sions through a trickster-like summoning of chaos. Her book *Mis/Takes* is a wonderful reading of such challenging films as *Mulholland Drive, Memento,* and *The Others.*[20]

Whereas Beebe and Waddell focus on art as disturbance, John Izod, in *Screen, Culture, Psyche,*[21] and Terence Dawson in *The Effective Protagonist in the Nineteenth-Century British Novel,*[22] both emphasize psychic integration. Dawson's is an original and highly satisfying post-Jungian theory of the novel, in which meaning engages in a process toward wholeness. The journey towards psychic integration focuses on the text and then provides healing in author and reader. On a collective level, the novel's long career in society aids social and cultural integration.

Dawson's stress on wholeness indicates that he regards Jung as a structuralist whose ideas tend towards relatively stable meaning.[23] This characterization of Jung as structuralist emphasizes Jungian psychology as a *model* (see Chapter 1), organized by dualistic forces and proposing archetypes as centering energies that promote relatively stable forms and significance. What makes Dawson's structuralist Jung stand out, however, is his refusal to lapse into essentialism. Although Dawson reads novels for psychic wholeness, his conception of wholeness is incarnate in time, and therefore historically contingent and shaped by cultural understanding.

His fascinating innovation is the trope of the "effective protagonist." This is the one figure in a novel to whom the psychic currents and images of the *whole text* relate. The effective protagonist is rarely the apparent hero of the story. In *Ivanhoe* by Sir Walter Scott, Dawson suggests that the effective protagonist is the hero's father. In a stunning revision of *Wuthering Heights,* the effective protagonist is revealed as Catherine Linton, daughter to both the ill-fated beloveds, Cathy and Edgar Linton. If Jung locates art on the creative border between order and chaos, Dawson shows some of the potential of emphasizing art's ordering and integrative possibilities.

John Izod's work has explored film's power for making myth dynamically real, in addition to developing a post-Jungian stance on the film audience. While not denying the political and ideological aspects of myth in film, Izod uncovers what much conventional film criticism neglects: myth's psychological numinosity. For example, he brings new resonance to the perennial topic of the hero in the collective imagination. Heroes, he writes,

... convey to the enthralled congregation in the cinema's darkened arena something of the numinous intensity previously invested in the human gods of organized religion.[24]

Luke Hockley is another pioneer who has brought Jungian ideas of the creative unconscious to bear on the emotional, social, and psychological impact of film.[25] He has also suggested that archetypal images provide a way of understanding film genres.[26] As with archetypes themselves, there is no actual "ur-text" for film genres such as the Western, no perfect template that all subsequent examples must follow. Rather, there are collections of films bearing resemblances to each other, which we agree to characterize by genre.

Returning to Izod's work, he also outlines a significant debate for post-Jungian media critics and perhaps for all the arts. Is there any longer a real division between high "art" and popular media? If so, how does such a division affect consideration of the numinous creativity of the unconscious? Izod puts it very clearly by stating that all films must be regarded as carriers of symbolic energy originating in the collective consciousness and unconscious.[27]

Such a strong position on the role of the unconscious in today's media is potentially controversial. Izod moves to the important territory of cultural analysis by looking at the role of non-artistic factors, such as media corporations. Commercial cinema has let money-making values seep into, and arguably sour, the sphere of art. Some Jungians might suggest, archetypally speaking, that the Jungian senex/puer pairing of figures—senex, the "old man," representing maturity and wisdom, and puer standing for youthful imagination and risk-taking—have become unbalanced and distorted. The senex figure thus becomes cynical and exploitative.

So in blockbuster movies, made by a senex Hollywood culture *for* adolescents (whether chronological or psychological), we have a "culture of senex inculcating the puer."[28] Izod prefers instead those mainstream films where an auteur director can still manifest the Jungian Self, such as Stanley Kubrick's *Barry Lyndon* and *Eyes Wide Shut*. On the vexed matter of global commercial cinema, Jungian theorist Don Fredericksen has devoted a searching critical energy to the popular culture debate. I will consider his views shortly.

Jungian Arts Theory and its Debates

To sum up post-Jungian arts theory is to discover two historical movements. Outside the purely clinical sphere of the therapies, Jungian arts criticism first of all tended to use Jungian concepts in order to provide a uniquely "Jungian" perspective on literature, film, etc. These determined Jungians risked taking over-emphasizing the logos element (see Chapters 1 and 2) of transcendent, conceptual separateness.

Such critics, often called liberal humanists, risked treating Jung's writings as *essentialist*, that is, as proposing fixed, non-historically conditioned truths about human nature and art. This approach to art believes that a common human nature surmounts any local historical effects: art always transcends the contingent and particular. My basic challenge to Jungian criticism in essentialist mode it is that it is *not Jungian enough*.

For Jung himself, in all his writing, such as on James Joyce's *Ulysses*, took art supremely seriously as witness to *the creative psyche in historical time*. What is most intensely *Jungian* is his insistence on the primacy of the partly unknowable creative unconscious. Therefore essentialism is anathema. Art is historically embedded (immanent) in culture, and an artwork will change over time with its audiences in different cultural conditions; yet history does not determine art. Art *does* participate in transcendence, in the unknowable. But transcendence is only accessible *from known ground*. So a second, more authentically *Jungian* arts criticism arises, one that refuses to treat Jungian ideas as a means of *fully knowing art*. It respects transcendence in unknowability and also recognizes art's embodiment in history.

Such a contemporary Jungian approach is also aware of adjacent historical factors, including other theoretical approaches. For example, Dawson and Izod recognize cultural materialism but refute the restricting essentialism of historical materialism. My own work has proposed re-working Jung's psychological and visionary perspectives as *forms of reading* (see above), and a new Jungian reader-response theory.[29] I have also, like others, sought to bring Jung and the work of Jacques Derrida together.[30] Perhaps the critic who has done most so far to show how Jungian ideas can ameliorate problems in existing cultural theory is Don Fredericksen. His critique centers on the popular culture debate.

Debating Aesthetic Value: Is Popular Culture a Home for the Symbol-Making Unconscious, or a Cynical Manipulation of Archetypes into Stereotypes?

In the very useful 2001 collection of essays, *Jung and Film*, Fredericksen gives an invaluable account of the existing state of mainstream non-Jungian film criticism.[31] Three primary theoretical sources—the writings of Roland Barthes, Jacques Lacan, and Karl Marx—have led to the development of critical theories well suited to dissecting the political and social dimension of film. However, all three critical perspectives are deficient in accounting for film's symbolic resonance.

Fredericksen bases his position on Jung's distinction between signs and symbols, signs standing for the knowable and symbols for the in-part unknowable or not yet known. In turn, this binary division produces Jung's categories of psychological and visionary art. Fredericksen believes these categories hold good for modern cinema. Visionary cinema carries the potential for the Jungian Self to flower in the film through the auteur director. An illuminating example is given in Fredericksen's stunning analysis of Ingmar Bergman's *Persona*.[32] Blockbuster cinema, by contrast, is so corrupted by commerce that it merely flattens the imagination. The resulting films are banal and, indeed, *harm* the collective psyche. In "Stripping Bare the Images,"[33] Fredericksen goes much further than Izod and other critics in disowning Hollywood, arguing that blockbusters actively try to harness the creative power of myths and symbols in cynical attempts to "hook" unsophisticated minds. Joseph Campbell, for example, was a mythographer much influenced by Jung, and his *The Hero with a Thousand Faces*[34] has been plundered by manuals offering formulas for successful films, in particular Christopher Vogler's *The Writer's Journey*.[35]

Here it is not so much a question of art corrupted by the saturation of money, but of an ever more dominant media draining away the creative potency of its audience. Fredericksen is only, perhaps, the most dedicated of those post-Jungian critics who fear that all new technology, including the internet, stupefies rather than engages the human psyche. He calls for a critical challenge, a fight to lure the mindful hearts and heartened minds of the public away from an addictive media that exploits myth to fake depth. What is needed now, Fredericksen suggests, is a new asceticism, a renunciation of symbolism in the hope that art can become art again. Otherwise we are trapped in popular culture as the organ of capitalist colonialism of the soul.

Such a diagnosis of popular culture is persuasive. Indeed, I am more and more persuaded by it! However, not all post-Jungian critics agree with Fredericksen. Some, myself included, have tried to argue that however cynical and formulaic is the making process of blockbusters, a spark of the Jungian creative unconscious is never quite extinguished. However politically and socially pernicious a film appears, it is nevertheless made by people whose unconscious is never wholly in their control. So even in the most abject of examples, some creativity inevitably remains autonomous and can be rescued. Put simply, Hollywood corruption cannot wholly pervade meaning because the creative and partly unknowable unconscious is never *completely* overwhelmed.

An interesting example of a counter-position to Fredericksen is Don Williams's essay on *Bladerunner* in *Jung and Film*.[36] In that interesting category of films that appear mainstream yet also bear a director's individual imprint, *Bladerunner* deals with symptomatic issues of imagination, humanity, otherness, and the post-human. Williams shows that the film, while citing clichés of film noir, etc., actually re-invigorates such tropes as romance, the hardboiled cop, the inhuman villain, and even religious ideas of origins and self. In this film, myths of individuation condense around the relations between the apparently human characters and the evidently non-human replicants. Pity, love, and sympathy are portrayed in ways at once intensely familiar and profoundly imaginative. Such a reading does not dispose of Fredericksen's powerful indictment of formulaic blockbuster cinema. It does, however, suggest that despite the dominance of capitalism in the arts, there are margins where artists are actively addressing the problem.

Fredericksen believes that Hollywood capitalism is so totalizing that the unconscious cannot live there. So complex is it that it has acquired a kind of artificial intelligence. It is able to fake the collective unconscious by mining mythical writing for flat, pat, denatured meanings. From archetypes to stereotypes, popular culture has become identical with commerce. This takes what Jung feared about modernity, its hyper-rationalism, and twists it into a parody of his remedy, the re-vitalizing of myth.

Seeking to eradicate individuality, cultural capitalism substitutes dead myths for Jung's collective unconscious. But can genuine, psychically dynamic myth survive the technological age? What is the future for Jung's view of myth as a vitalizing narrative of the psyche?

Here we will need to look at Jung on myth and history. Such a perspective is the subject of Chapter 4.

FURTHER READING

Jung as Critic of the Arts
C.G. Jung, "*Ulysses*: a Monologue," "On the Relation of Analytical Psychology to Poetry," "Psychology and Literature," in *The Spirit in Man, Art and Literature, The Collected Works of C.G. Jung*, vol. 15, trans. R.F.C. Hull (Princeton, NJ: Princeton University Press, 1932).

   These three essays are provocative and challenging on the relationship between the arts and psychology. "*Ulysses*..." is a magnificent work of criticism as comedy!

Key Post-Jungian Arts Criticism (Literature and Film)
James Baumlin, Tita F. Baumlin, and George Jensen, *Post-Jungian Criticism* (New York: State University of New York Press, 2004).

   A strong and varied collection of Jungian criticism showing a developing field.

John Beebe, "The Trickster in the Arts," *San Francisco Jung Institute Library Journal*, vol. 2, no. 2 (1981): 48.

   This essay deserves to be heralded as the start of a new sophistication in Jungian arts criticism. It superbly combines analytical skills and artistic sensitivity. It is a model for future practice.

Edmund Cusick, "Psyche and the Artist: Jung and the Poet," in Rowland (2008), pp. 12-21.

   The late Edmund Cusick was an inspired critic of poetry as well as a very fine poet in his own right.

Terence Dawson, *The Effective Protagonist in the Nineteenth-Century British Novel: Scott, Brontë, Eliot, Wilde* (London: Ashgate, 2004).

   An innovative and highly original critic of literature from a Jungian perspective, Dawson specializes in impeccably researched cultural history as it intersects with, and is illuminated by, Jungian psychology.

Don Fredericksen, "Jung/Sign/Symbol/Film," in Hauke and Alister (2001), pp. 17-55.

Don Fredericksen, *Bergman's Persona* (Poznan: Wydawnictwo Naukowe, 2005).

Don Fredericksen, "Stripping Bare the Images," in Rowland (2008).

Don Fredericksen has done much to establish Jungian film studies. He is a trenchant cultural critic and a powerful advocate for the imagination in/of film.

Christopher Hauke and Ian Alister, eds., *Jung and Film: Post-Jungian Takes on the Moving Image* (London and New York: Routledge, 2001).

This essay collection has been hugely influential, so much so that a second one is planned for 2011, this time edited by Christopher Hauke and Luke Hockley.

Luke Hockley, "*Film Noir:* Archetypes or Stereotypes?" in Hauke and Alister (2001), pp. 177-193.

Like Fredericksen and Izod, Luke Hockley is one of the pioneers of Jungian film theory, continually offering new insights and areas of critical focus. Hockley's work cannot be missed.

John Izod, *Screen, Culture, Psyche: A Post-Jungian Approach to Working with the Audience* (London and New York: Routledge, 2006).

Susan Rowland, *C.G. Jung and Literary Theory: The Challenge from Fiction* (London: Palgrave, 1999).

This book begins to link Jung to literary theory and to contemporary British novelists.

Susan Rowland, ed., *Psyche and the Arts: Jungian Approaches to Music, Architecture, Literature, Painting and Film* (London and New York: Routledge, 2008).

A diverse collection of Jungian arts criticism, this has some surprising and unusual pieces, such as on the poetry of a Brazilian classroom.

Terrie Waddell, *Mis/Takes: Archetype, Myth and Identity in Screen Fiction* (London and New York: Routledge, 2006).

> Waddell is a highly persuasive critic with some excellent readings of some of the most perplexing of modern films. She is beginning to extend the potential of Jungian ideas in film in a very interesting direction.

Don Williams, "'If You Could See What I've Seen With Your Eyes ... ': Post-Human Psychology and *Blade Runner*," in Hauke and Alister (2001), pp. 110-28.

> This moving essay is a testament to how the mainstream cinema can sometimes incarnate both depth and mystery. All Jungian film critics can learn from Williams's weaving together of analyst and critic in his perspective.

Significant Works of Art Influenced by Jungian Ideas

Margaret Atwood, *Alias Grace* (London: Bloomsbury, 2006).

> All of Atwood's work shows the presence of an underground Jungian current. This novel is a more overt consideration of the evolution of the anima, one dedicated, moreover, to providing "her" point of view.

Lindsay Clarke, *The Chymical Wedding* (New York: Ballantine, 1989), *Alice's Masque* (London: Picador, 1995).

> These two novels combine myth, history, and the contemporary world in ways that are lasting gifts to the reader's imagination.

Lindsay Clarke, *The War at Troy* (New York: Thomas Dunne Books, 2004), *The Return From Troy* (London: HarperCollins, 2006).

> Clarke not only re-writes the *Iliad* and the *Odyssey* in Jungian terms, he is inspired to blend novel and epic in a tour de force of literary art.

Edmund Cusick, *Ice Maidens* (Liverpool: Headland Press, 2006).

> Here are poems on love, sex, spirituality, social embarrassment, wild nature, and even wilder women. A wonderful contemporary evocation of the anima.

Doris Lessing, *The Marriages Between Zones Three, Four and Five* (London: Grafton, 1983).
   Another novelist whose work has absorbed Jungian ideas, Lessing famously told critics that this novel began as an "active imagination."

Michele Roberts, *In the Red Kitchen* (London: Methuen, 1990).
   This feminist novel critically examines the way both Freudians and Jungians have treated women, and a very brief appearance by C.G. Jung is the joke that confirms it.

George Lucas, *Star Wars* (1977).

John Boorman, *Excalibur* (1981), *The Emerald Forest* (1985).

Myth and History

A Problem with Myth?

The most significant professional association of Jung's career was with the founder of psychoanalysis, Sigmund Freud.[1] It ended in bitterness and acrimony in 1913 after Jung published a book on symbols, in which he departed from Freud's fierce contention that all psychic energy is sexual in origin. Partly as a result of this traumatic moment in his life, Jung had a breakdown from which he later drew inspiration.

Jung tells, in *Memories, Dreams, Reflections* (hereafter *MDR*),[2] of how he began a habit of debating with himself. Later this becomes a sense of being challenged by the voices of *others* within himself. At this point, his inner debate is about what he has or has not achieved with his work. He has written a book explaining the symbols of myths, but does this mean, he wonders, that myths have now been explained *away*?[3] It seems to him that the modern person has no myth because he or she has no sense of participating in a living story that gives meaning to life. Jung then asks himself whether he himself has a myth, a structure or story capable of shaping and creating meaning for his life and his Self.[4]

The key chapter of *MDR*, "Confrontation with the Unconscious," shows Jung's inner struggles providing the *matter* from which he evolves a

"personal myth." This is, first of all, a personal story, his psychic autobiography. It is then amplified into "his" psychology, Jungian psychology, his
theories given to the world. Crucially, his psychology as "personal myth"
signifies the indivisible union of his ideas and his personal story. Explicitly,
his life's work is presented as embedded in a personal and historical world.

In Jungian psychology, personal myth is an autobiographical formation presented in a dialogical relationship with the theoretical side of his
psychology, which is necessarily conceptual and thus transcendent of
the contingencies of autobiography. Elsewhere I have characterized his
work as *personal myth in dialogue with grand theory.*[5] Here "grand theory"
or "grand narrative" refers to universal ideas not local to any particular
culture. Grand narratives purport to *explain* history.

This chapter will investigate Jung's use of the term "myth" an as
element integral both to the shaping of individual and collective human
life, and to the shaping of ideas. It will show Jung's treatment of myth
to be at once a radical and a traditional variant of myth's long history.
This will lead us to consider Jung's vision of history and its psychological significance. Indeed, much of Jung's devotion to myth is in the cause
of *re-shaping history into psychic energy,* though a process of meaning-
making. Jung's myth builds history *into* the individual soul.

Freud and Jung: Oedipus is Complex!

In 1909, when Freud and Jung were about to embark for America, Jung
made an offhand remark that provoked a crisis between them. Recalling
that ancient dead bodies were being recovered from northern European
bogs, Jung momentarily confused them with discoveries of mummies in
lead-lined German cellars. Freud was not amused; indeed, his reaction
was so strong that he fainted. Later accusing Jung of harboring a death
wish towards him, Freud insisted that an Oedipal narrative was being
played out between the two men.

According to the Freudian theory of the Oedipus complex, the myth
treated in Sophocles' play *Oedipus Rex* has resonated down through the
centuries because it represents an inner drama of the origins of every
man. The Greek Oedipus flees his childhood home because an oracle has
foretold that he will kill his father and have sex with his mother. Travel-

ing alone, Oedipus meets a quarrelsome man at a crossroads. He kills him and enters the nearby city of Thebes, which he discovers is being ravaged by a monster, the Sphinx.

By answering a riddle posed by the Sphinx, Oedipus saves the city (or so it appears) and is hailed a hero. He is rewarded with the hand in marriage of its widowed queen, and so becomes king. Only years later, after his children are born, does Oedipus find out the horrific truth about his own parentage. Turned out to die as a baby and fostered by another ruler, it is his own father he killed at the crossroads on the way to Thebes, and his own mother who is Queen of Thebes and the mother of his children.

To Freud, Oedipus's actions trace the archaic desires of the boy baby. The newborn is first entirely fixated on the mother as source of his being; infant sexuality is mother-directed. As soon as the boy-child realizes that there is an unwelcome third in the family, the father, he experiences a murderous rage. He wants to eliminate the threat to his exclusive access to the mother. Then, upon the hazy and chaotic realization that the mother's body is different, has no penis, he suddenly comes to fear that the father may castrate him just as he appears to have done to the mother. The only safe option is to give up the sexual obsession with the all-embracing mother, and identify with the father in his gender.

Renouncing the love of the mother requires a splitting off of forbidden desires. That act of splitting from his deepest desires *creates* the unconscious as a psychic domain separate from ego. Founded upon sexual repression, the unconscious thus haunts masculine subjectivity as tabooed sexuality. Oedipus—to Freud, the one person in history who does not suffer the Oedipus complex because he *does what is forbidden*—remains the central and most significant myth in Freudian psychology.

Freud believed that, in fainting during the 1909 incident with Jung, his body had taken on the role of Oedipus' unfortunate father, Laius, with the younger Jung as the threatening, aggressive Oedipus. Though neither says as much, it would appear from the context that the "mother" whose body, whose *matter* they both desire exclusively is *psychoanalysis itself*. For they had *both* been invited to lecture in America, with Jung's invitation implicitly challenging Freud's superior, "paternal" status.

Freud's insistence on interpreting Jung's words as representing a death wish is contrary to Jung's own preferred method of interpretation by analogy. Idly chatting, Jung finds his thoughts moving from bog bodies to mummies in cellars. What links these two examples of the long-dead is the preservation of the body (deliberate in the case of the mummies, natural in bogs); what separates them is that the bog bodies were all murdered (scholars assume that either the bog victims were either executed criminals or ritual sacrifices to a fierce earth goddess). When Freud faints in Jung's arms, his body is afflicted by *difference*. Jung, on the other hand, is giving an early example of what will become one of his key epistemological strategies, that of *incorporation*. He is making an idea or generating significance through cultural analogy. Here, in what he will later come to call "active imagination," one image (bog bodies) is allowed to unconsciously develop (into mummies in cellars).

So how do these different types of making meaning affect the interpretation of the Oedipus myth? Needless to say, Jung's view of Oedipus, the hero, is a little different from that of Freud. He focuses on an aspect of the myth barely mentioned by Sophocles, the Sphinx—part woman, part winged lion. To Jung, Oedipus *fails* to conquer the Sphinx, and therein sows his own disaster. True, Oedipus does give a clever reply to the Sphinx's riddle of what goes on four legs, then two legs, then three legs (answer: man). However, this easy intellectual triumph is no true answer to such a complex being as the Sphinx.

For she, in her animal-human-divine form, is the true primal Mother, the true archaic origin to whom a mere tribute of intellect is nothing at all. Oedipus fails to realize, fails to *make real to himself,* the original chaos that the Sphinx represents. Hence he will be horribly cursed in the matter of origins and birth. To Jung, the Oedipus myth is one where the hero fails his true task of separating from the unconscious, falling into the unconscious by merging with the mother. Having initially failed to discover his own (familial) boundaries, Oedipus is finally destroyed by being forced to see that he is both son and lover.

What is integral to Jung's Oedipus myth is that it remains a *myth*. The Sphinx in her chaotic multiplicity (human, animal, divine) bears the potential for many stories. Indeed, there are many possible ways of being a hero. If Oedipus had been capable of truly separating from her, the Sphinx as the primal Great Mother might have meant more for him than annihilation. "She" could also have energized his rebirth *from* her.

In that harsh short exchange between Freud and Jung, there are two possible approaches to interpreting myth. Is a myth *one story*, so neatly repeatable that it can be translated directly into an abstract concept such as the Oedipus complex? Or is it rather a story possessed of such psychic energy (not always confined to sexual energy) that it is inevitably *many stories*? Are myths perhaps technologies for making *meanings that cannot be separated from their stories*? We are asking whether myth is separate from history, offering a possible transcendent meaning. Or could myth be an immanent shaping story that is endlessly incorporative? Such a notion of myth within history does not separate myth out from embodied life, so it can never structure an-Other *outside* itself, that is, transcendent of historical, embodied experience.

Here is a story about myth and history.

The Problem of Myth and History

When the poet, Seamus Heaney, collected his Nobel Prize in 1994, he told the story of something that had happened during the violent "Troubles" between Protestants and Catholics in Northern Ireland in the 1970s.[6] A bus-load of workers had been stopped by masked gunmen, who made the workers, mostly Protestant, line up beside the road. "Any Catholics among you step forward," they ordered. Everyone assumed that these were Protestant paramilitaries out to kill Catholics. The one Catholic stepped forward. As he did so, however, he felt the touch of a hand pulling him back. One of his co-workers was saying to him, silently, with body language, "Don't go, we will protect you." It was too late. The man had stepped forward and was quickly thrust aside. Then all the other men standing in line were gunned down. It had been a Catholic gang, killing Protestants.

On the one hand, this terrible story illustrates what many cultural critics believe: that myth is, by its very nature, dangerous, and always politically suspect. Here are two communities, so similar that they cannot tell each other apart on sight. Yet they are divided absolutely by narratives, by myths of community membership that define each as absolutely Other. Protestant and Catholic, although ostensibly belonging to the same Christian religion, are here creatures of opposing myths; what flies between them are bullets. Furthermore, in this situation, it is not just religious myths which are dividing people; these two groups also have separate *historical* myths. Each community adheres to its own separate story of the past, stories that have congealed and now confine the present into a situation of complete community division.

Heaney's anecdote clearly shows that myth can structure a politics of opposition and violence. From the myth is abstracted a concept of identity, such as "Northern Irish Catholic" or "Protestant," that leaves no chink, no space to re-invent, to include or even connect to the Other. In such a situation, myth politicizes the understanding of history, becoming a source of stories that fix one identity by excluding another. This is the politics of myth as fascism.

Seamus Heaney is well aware of how toxic myth can become for his own Northern Irish communities. Yet his reaction is not to try to strip myth away from the understanding of present and past. Rather he aims to develop an-Other kind of myth, one that can build upon the single hopeful moment in his anecdote, the touch of the hand that goes beyond tribalism. This means invoking a sense of myth as inherently bearing other stories, as a *technology for making meanings*.

In order to truly understand the positions of Heaney, Freud and Jung, we now need to consider the long history of myth itself.

Theories of Myth

The Greek philosophers Plato and Aristotle held different attitudes to myth that have informed the word's usage down through the centuries.[7] These differences came to be regarded as the opposition of *logos* and *mythos*. I have dealt with these terms in Chapters 1 and 2. Now I want to revisit that earlier argument in order to deepen my analysis of myth.

In the logos sense, myth brings about—or can be made to produce— abstract ideas or knowledge. Plato believed that the ultimate reality was a transcendent realm of Forms, not directly accessible to the human mind. Trapped in a huge cave, mankind sees patterns in the shadows cast on the wall and takes them for truth. Only the hero-philosopher seeks the ultimate reality and tries to get outside to the sunshine, to the realm of clear, distinct ideas, the domain of repeatable truth, that is, to the logos. Logos as truth *exceeds* the story, the myth that contains it, and can be extracted. As Laurence Coupe puts it, myth has thus been domesticated.[8] Myth is now allegory.

By contrast, Aristotle regarded narrative as dynamic and energizing. Mythos, or story, is *emplotment within the telling of history*, in that we inevitably recount historical events as a kind of narrative. Hence myth *inhabits* the writing of history; myth is not a "form" extractable from it. This approach to myth is not allegorical, because it generates nothing outside itself; its form has no Other. There is not "history" as the "truth" about the past and "myths" as fictions belonging to another realm. Rather, mythos is a recurring story that shapes meaning without recourse to anything else. Myth as mythos, rather than as logos, does not refer to or seek out some kind of primal truth. There is no ur-myth, no superior narrative that will divide up reality neatly and without remainder. Rather, myth is by its very nature endlessly re-inventive of identity and being.

So rather than characterize the touch of the hand in Heaney's story as a despairing gesture against harsh unyielding political reality, myth as mythos can *re-frame the meaning*. Myth can become the germ of a new story of Irish identity. Mythos offers stories as myths of becoming, embodied in history through the endless fertility of human desire. Of course, such a casting of myth as mythos welcomes the Jungian notion of the unconscious. Mythos individuates at a personal and social level and thereby renews a culture polarized by frozen allegories of identity.

To take further this examination, I turn to Coupe's reformulation of Greek logos and mythos as *allegory* and *radical typology*, respectively.[9] The Christian Church, as an institution, tended to take Christian myth *allegorically*, regarding the Christian story as capable of generating fixed truths wholly separable from their lived context. In such a way, the Church produced absolute doctrine and abstract truth. However, this is not the only way to treat Christianity. Jesus often taught through parables, stories that generate ever more meanings without fixing any one. Other types of religion and religious thought—from shamanism to mystical, revolutionary doctrines such as that of poet William Blake—have espoused an eternal dialogical relationship between sacred and profane, rather than a singular strategy of abstraction from the imperfect, the secular, and the bodily. Here the sacred is not transcendent, not constructed from myth by allegory, but rather is immanent, found within the profane. The sacred is structured by the dynamism of myth as mythos, as comprising inherently multiple stories. Coupe describes Blake's visionary sense of the divine:

> A Christian, but a highly unorthodox one, Blake set himself the task of revitalizing the Christian myth; indeed, he was one of the first believers to conjecture that the story of Jesus really was a liberating myth, not a literal truth. Far from seeing the bible as the last word—indeed, the ultimate Word—he felt able to rewrite it totally according to the dictates of his imagination, which he took to be a spiritual force. [10]

Coupe calls this sense of myth as incarnate in body and history "radical typology," because it resembles a Medieval method of studying the Bible known as *typological reading*, which looked for *types* of Christ-like events elsewhere than in the story of Christ himself. Mythos is *radical typology* because it is not trying to discover any particular story; it has no prior bias to substantiate. Medieval typology was really another way of allegorizing Christian truth from myth. Radical typology sees the recurrence of mythic stories as generative of meaning without presupposing any singular meaning. Radical typology/mythos is a way of exploring that is always looking out for new meanings. By contrast, allegory/logos is a way of stabilizing meanings. Put another way, allegory/logos makes meaning by *separating out* truth from story, matter, body, and history, while radical typology/mythos makes meaning by *shaping from within* story, matter, body, and history.

Allegory works towards myth as transcendence, and as such is an agent of the Sky Father. Radical typology/mythos is *meaning achieved through incarnation*—through matter, body and sexuality, through intuition (connecting to the Other within, the unconscious), through immersion in history and desire; Earth Mother is thus served by radical typology.

I am arguing that these two approaches to myth, allegory and radical typology, also function as two types of consciousness, and ultimately that these two types of consciousness *themselves have a mythical origin*. The two main types of world creation myth would appear to sponsor, on the one hand, the stories behind rational logos consciousness, with its emphasis on *separation* from the Other, and on the other hand, the multivalent myths of a mythos consciousness which *connects* with the Other.

Ann Baring and Jules Cashford, in their comprehensive history of myths of the feminine divine, *The Myth of the Goddess*,[11] write that the earliest type of religious myth seems to be of an earth goddess. She represents the sacred as immanent within nature and world. She gives birth to all life, including human beings. As prior to gender division, she contains both genders, and generates no structure that can be Other to either one of them. She stands for the divine as sexuality, embodiment, eros, connection, feeling, and love. She signifies a plurality of meanings because she refuses to separate any out.

Her incarnation can also be described as animism, the goddess as sacred nature in every tree, brook, or mountain. She speaks in many voices, woven together in a net or tapestry that forbids the privileging of any *one*. She bears the understanding of myth as mythos.

Ancient history suggests that a long period of earth goddess worship was succeeded by a dramatic shift in consciousness by the arrival of a new type of god. These "Sky Fathers" eventually developed into the one masculine transcendent god of monotheism in Judaism, Christianity, and Islam, who exists separately from his creation. Earth, nature, and man are completely distinct from the sacred.

"Man" formed in the image of "God" shares some of the latter's divine transcendence of nature, body, matter. The habit of separation, characteristic of Sky Fathers, begins with gender, so masculinity itself becomes associated with transcendence, separation, and rational discriminating consciousness. Yet these very qualities are formed by dividing off from femininity as matter, body, sexuality, nature, and earth.

Whereas the son of the goddess seeks union in a sacred marriage with divine nature, the son of the Sky Father is entrusted with a mission to renounce the body and the feminine. He must seek spirit as divorced from body, from the unconscious and its desires. He tries to rise above nature because it is always inferior to the logos for which he quests.

The mythologist, Joseph Campbell, wrote the hugely influential book on the hero myth, *The Hero with a Thousand Faces*,[12] which examines the many worldwide forms of the story of the young man who must separate from his mother, go on a dangerous quest, conquer a monster, and who is finally rewarded with the hand of the princess and a leadership role in his community. Such a story is ubiquitous because it is a narrative of the making of the human ego. We all have to separate from the body of the mother, experience aloneness as our ego builds, learn to repress or accommodate the unconscious, find a sexual union with another, and establish a position in our communities.

Campbell's work, however, assumes a male hero. Perhaps this is why he emphasizes the Sky Father pattern: ego generation by separation. Less is said about the Earth Mother hero pattern of making the ego through eros and connection. As a result, even Campbell, whose work is rooted in Jung's psychology, partook of what Jung realized was modernity's dangerous over-privileging of the masculine rational ego. A rational ego is not a problem in itself; rationality is clearly necessary, as long as it is not the *only* myth structuring consciousness. It becomes problematic when repressing the unconscious Other, when masculine separateness is gained at the expense of feminine eros.

One way of clarifying the problem of modern consciousness is to notice how far scientific reason *is a continuation of,* not a break from, Christian allegory and transcendence. As Lynn White, Jr. has argued, the logos of abstract scientific truth is constructed on the model of the masculine transcendent Sky Father.[13] Early Christian theologians agreed that God was not to be found in nature. "He" made the world and nature as entirely separate from "Himself," so nature was empty of meaning.

Knowledge was therefore envisioned as *abstractable* and *separable* from the matter of the world. Some theologians dedicated themselves to studying the natural world in order to discern, not the *presence*, but the *hand* of the Creator there, for surely Logos, the Word, the mind of God, would consist of rational concepts, categories, and natural laws. Eventually, scholars in this tradition redefined themselves as scientists, and gradually faith in God became optional. The object of study remained the logos, yet now the logos was the universal, abstract, rational truth of modernity's science.

The overzealous pursuit of logos in Western history is one dimension of the hardening of the Western ego. Indeed, the growth of the power of science could be understood mythically as the expansion of the hero myth. Abstract science is a heroic enterprise under the sign of the Sky Father, wresting "truth" from recalcitrant nature.

Feminist science fiction writer, Ursula K. Le Guin, has suggested as much in an evocative and engaging essay, "The Carrier Bag Theory of Fiction."[14] Le Guin speculates about the possible origins of culture itself as a way of contrasting the two gendered forms of the hero and creation myths. The earliest human artifacts found are usually spear points, which surely indicate a practice of hunting. We imagine our ancestors tracking animals through forests and plains. They must have lived a life of danger and excitement. With only simple spears to face large and resourceful prey, the outcome of the typical hunting expedition was far from a foregone conclusion. So our grandfathers of the hunting trail must have had some wonderful stories to tell!

The hunting story likely became the backbone of the tradition of tale-telling around the campfire. It is therefore a straightforward antecedent of the masculine hero myth. Of course, the aboriginal hunter must survive by repressing the Other. It is "kill or be killed" when facing a mammoth! However, Le Guin wonders, is this type of story *the only one* to originate from our earliest cultures? Suppose, she suggests, we think seriously about the first cultural objects and allow ourselves to envision two tales rather than one. Fundamentally, Le Guin is challenging *oneness*, monotheistic thinking, in the cause of *difference*, or plurality.

For even before spears were fashioned, people must have been using leaves to make a cup in order to drink water from the stream. Or they made a net for fish or to carry food, a bag to sling the baby in when gathering berries (a far greater part of the diet than meat). Alongside the culture of the spear point and hunting is the culture of the carrier bag. Less dramatic and exciting, perhaps, but the bag puts things together that were not associated before. Bags are a kind of a "medicine bundle" in which what are vital are the relationships made *between* things.

The carrier bag is ultimately behind the literary form of the novel, a form distinguished by *relationships* between characters. True, novels may have heroes. However, what happens to heroes in novels is that they must relate to "others," and in doing so they and their worlds are changed.

Le Guin warns that logos science is dangerous if it takes the masculine ego-hero too far from its feminine eros Other. "Masculine" science is "heroic" in its stamping out of nature's claims to be considered sentient and feeling. Interrupt the hero myth, defeat him and prevent his total triumph over the Other, and you have the cultural form of *tragedy*, in which the hero *goes too far*. He becomes so separate that his world cannot tolerate him. He dies alone.

If the male hero myth as tragedy inhabits modern science, this perhaps accounts for the hubris behind the manufacturing of weapons of mass destruction. As the Christian version of the hero myth shows, one possible destination for the myth is that the tragic hero unleashes the annihilation of the Other: the Bible ends with the Book of Revelation, an apocalyptic ending to history.

Jung was one of many to notice the resemblance between Christian apocalypse and the devastation possible through nuclear and other weapons of mass destruction. *Answer to Job*,[15] his imaginative re-writing of the Biblical tale, expresses his fears that apocalyptic revelation is at hand in modernity's dark heart, that the repressed Other, darkened by its very exclusion, will defeat the fragile ego. Hell will indeed be let loose!

In the next chapter on science and religion, I will show how Jung builds on the radical typological possibilities of myth in embodied history to re-make modernity's Christian/scientific framework through his notion of the Self. For now, I want to emphasize that, like Le Guin, Jung realizes the importance of the *two*. It is not a question of abolishing the masculine Sky Father, with his male ego hero myth of consciousness. Even if this were possible, it is not desirable.

The individual ego and human society are fostered by both types of consciousness, which entails both types of hero myth. Indeed, we must realize that Earth Mother and Sky Father are not only both necessary, *they are mutually constitutive*. Sky Father logos culture cannot exist without its Other and vice versa. So, unsurprisingly, even Christianity at its most patriarchal embraced Earth Mother images such as the Virgin Mother, her pose with the dying Christ replicating the ancient Mother Goddess clasping her son-lover.

As we saw in Chapter 1, Jung draws upon two types of myth in his psychological writings. Logos guards the rational concepts, while mythos situates them as embedded in the matter of body, psyche, history, and culture. His related notions of *eros* and *eros consciousness* represents feeling and connectedness (associated with mythos and the Earth Mother). Unfortunately, Jung's work is characterized by an unresolved conflict between misogynistic essentialism and radical cultural analysis when it comes to gender. This will be further examined in Chapter 6. Suffice to say that, on the one hand, he insists that there is no *innate gender* to the opposing forces of logos and eros, that both sexes need to develop both styles of consciousness. Yet he also tended to literalize his culturally biased perceptions of women's affinity to eros and supposed logos deficiencies in ways that obscure the profound mythical origin of these ideas.

Jung has a vision of myth as a vital shaping force in both the individual psyche and in history. Creation myth, far from a distant curiosity, is a living "matter" sponsoring forms of consciousness in the modern person. Modernity has produced many achievements by developing the Sky Father logos hero myth. Unfortunately, the fertile mutual embrace between the two myths—of transcendence and of immanence—has not been realized in modern culture.

In introducing such theoretical notions as logos and eros, and in the practice of writing itself, Jung was devoted to enacting a re-connection of the creation myths. By producing a psychology based upon the dialogical relation of personal myth and grand theory, his logos-writing creates an eros relation with the unconscious. In this, his psychology is *itself a radical typology mythos*, a re-writing of the dominant logos myth of his Christian heritage and the logos science he inherited from his studies.

Jung's attempt to restore the myths of consciousness to their proper fullness is in quest of wholeness for the modern psyche. To do this he wants *include eros* rather than to *eradicate logos*, neither dominating but rather supporting each other in a divine embrace of the psyche. One of the most pleasing and apparent examples of the interplay of logos and mythos in Jungian writing is the way he presents the two creation myths as necessary and mutual forms of consciousness.

In the next section I will return to Jung's quarrel with Freud to show logos and mythos—allegory and radical typology—at work in dialogical relationship in Jung's writing.

Freud and Jung (2): Oedipus Variations

Returning to Freud and Jung, the tiny episode over the bodies in bogs in 1909 comes to seem like a half-conscious anticipation of their ultimate quarrel. It fascinatingly reveals their preferences for different ways of construing myth.

Freud clearly prefers the allegorical method. He abstracts the Oedipus complex from the terrible fate of the mythical Oedipus. The Oedipus complex is a concept, universally applicable to the male psyche. His allegory is ultimately enriched, however, by an intimation of radical typology. This potential plenitude of stories inheres in that invention he is most famous for, the "talking cure" of psychoanalysis.

After all, although Freud believed—allegorically—that psychic energy was fundamentally sexual and resulted from the Oedipus complex, he also sought to enable tormented modern man to seek out *other stories*, other ways of living out the inevitable mythical Oedipal impulses graven deep in the soul. Where Freudian *theory* allegorizes the Oedipal myth to transcendent concept, Freudian clinical *practice* fosters a sense of creative immanence, of the many mythical stories embodied in our lives.

Jung's emphasis was different from the start. Preferring a radical typological or mythos approach, he was unable to agree with Freud that psychic energy was fundamentally sexual. To him, psychic energy was fundamentally *creative*; sexuality was only one of many possible expressions for the impulses of the soul. Myth *had* to be regarded as immanent, plural, capable of endless re-writing in an individual life. Myth, as narratives of psychic individuation, ceaselessly aims to connect to the Other, without ever appropriating it.

With his preference for a radical typological approach, *myth as non-foundational narrative* became crucial to Jung's psychology in three ways. Firstly, it could best represent the relations between ego and unconscious because it enacted their liminal, mutually constituting dialogue. Concepts, on the other hand, could only be of secondary value because they belonged to the ego alone. Secondly, myth does more than represent psychic relations; it also shapes them. So myth can be a healing intervention into a psyche that needs the structuring effect of a story in order to become less chaotic. Finally, as I will explore in more detail below, myth is a method of connecting the individual person to society, to the collective conscious and unconscious.

To give a last mention to hapless Oedipus, it is worth returning to Jung's contention that this hero's fatal mistake was to assume that he had conquered the Sphinx by cleverness. Oedipus invites catastrophe because he assumes that rational intellect can solve the problem of the Other. He fails to understand his story as containing both types of myth. He falls into extreme, blind, unconscious literalism, living out murderous and incestuous desires, which blinds him both to a Freudian sort of allegorical conceptual comprehension of his situation *and* to a more Jungian sense of radical typological mythos, in which the terrifying chaos of the Sphinx is recognized as a limitless source of understanding.

Just as Freud emphasizes logos yet necessarily also finds a integral role for mythos, so Jung stresses mythos yet concedes a pivotal role for logos. With regard to the Oedipus myth, Jung always agreed that the Oedipus complex played a role in the psyche. He differed from Freud in believing that it was only important for *some* patients, not universally for the male psyche. Of course, the evident role of mythical allegory or logos in Jung's work is to be found in his favored concepts of unconscious, shadow, anima, compensation, teleology, and so on.

My argument is that Jung's allegorical logos is explicitly in dialogue with his preference for radical typology mythos *because he is ultimately trying to re-balance the creation myths in modernity*. Why this is such an important task, we will consider shortly when looking at Jung's views of history. A clue comes from the bog itself. In the fateful exchanges between the two men, Freud unconsciously makes a radical typology sort of move in acting out "Laius" by bodily inscribing the myth story as death (alleging that Jung has the Oedipal death wish). By contrast, Jung's attitude to death by sacrifice is that it can be radically typologically understood as presaging rebirth.

Oedipus in the myth is cast out on a hillside to die, yet survives with the help of shepherds. If Freud could have taken his limited acceptance of radical typology further, and if Jung had considered more deeply the significance of Freud's adherence to modernity's logos, what might have been possible for a depth psychology *re-united in a rebirth from the bog?*

Jung's "Historical Novel" and Shakespeare's *The Tempest*[16] as "Future History"

Jung's most complete example of history writing is *Aion*.[17] I suggest that *Aion* works best when understood as a "historical nonfiction novel." What do I mean by this? The book is a history of the European imagination through symbolic forms of time and space, and is therefore more than history in the usual sense. By deploying the historically potent images of Gnosticism, astrology, alchemy, Christianity, modern physics, etc., Jung is not only writing *about* the history of European symbolic culture, he is *enacting* it. *Aion* is the textual embodiment of the many voices that constitute European consciousness through time and in space.

Moreover, in writing that lays bare the inter-animation of symbolic systems (for example, how Pisces astrology becomes part of Christian iconography and vice versa), *Aion* is designed to stir into life the animistic multiplicity of the reader's psyche. This textual animism is energized in dialogue with the ego's need for coherence of meaning. Again we see in Jung's writing the mythical web of unconscious expression through symbolism, made intelligible in a dialogue with logos rational argument and concepts. Here, in the coherent focus on the history of psychic systems of symbols, the text works similarly to the way Le Guin describes the novel: figures animated through relating to each other and to the reader. So *Aion* is the *reader's* "historical novel": through the power of the Jungian symbol, the reader is dialogically woven into history.

To Jung, history is not a coherent story, for if it were, it would risk becoming a transcendent myth of culture. For Jung, history is psychic energy, understandable only through a dialogical inter-animation of radical typology and allegory. By such means, the telling of history regains a dimension of immanence, of embodied, erotic life, taking on the characteristics of a historical *novel*, of a form of imaginative enchantment. The historical time and cultural space of symbols are woven into the bodies, psyches, and individuating stories of its readers. Jung's history is continually written and re-written as symbolic stories (myths) plait the individual into the collective. For Jung, history *is* the complex of mythos that links the individual to the space-time of culture and history.

The Tempest and Future History

In *Aion*, Jung remarks that the European Renaissance was a crucial turning point in history because there was a fundamental re-orientation of space and time.[18] Previously, the cultural psyche had been devoted to "heights," to the medieval Gothic striving for spiritual transcendence. In the Renaissance, there was a turn to horizontal journeying in voyages of exploration, along with which came a drive for "the conquest of nature."[19] Jung could easily have added that voyages of exploration cast a forward shadow of future colonialism. Conquest of the Other was to occur as conquest of territory, of peoples, of nature, and of the psyche.

So it might be interesting to consider a Renaissance text, Shakespeare's *The Tempest*, in the light of Jung's understanding of changes in cultural direction. Also relevant is Jung's belief (see Chapter 3) that some visionary works of art carry the teleological future orientation of the psyche. Where *Aion* looks back at cultural symbolic understanding of time-space from the twentieth century, can we see a symbolic dimension to *The Tempest* directed toward the future? If Jung's history is mythos linking the individual to the collective, then can *The Tempest* be "future history"?

The Play

Named for a meteorological event, *The Tempest* is structured around both painful intersections of physical existence in place and the torturing possibilities of time. Although he is living on an island supplying all his physical needs, Prospero is not happy. Once he was Duke of Milan, but he had been deposed by his own brother—in part, at least, because Prospero had neglected the business of ruling in favor of his fascination with magic.

Cast adrift on a boat with his baby daughter, Miranda, Prospero is shipwrecked on an inhabited island, where he develops into a powerful magician. His sorcery is elemental, giving him control of land and sea. An image of his capacity to rule through learned magic is made substantial in the figure of Caliban, a dark native whom he enslaves. Thus Prospero's island anticipates European colonialism. Prospero interferes with indigenous power struggles in freeing the "airy spirit," Ariel, who had been imprisoned in a cloven pine by Caliban's witch mother, Sycorax. Unfortunately, Prospero's apparent act of emancipation is merely a change of service, for Ariel, along with Caliban, becomes Prospero's bound servant—the *imprisoned spiritual energy* of colonial transformation of the island.

To Prospero, Caliban is brute, dark matter, a slave fit only for menial work. Not surprisingly, he is treated with more disdain than delicate Ariel. True, Caliban tried to rape the now-adolescent Miranda. But the play forbids the development of a hybrid post-colonial culture, offspring of Caliban and Miranda, in the very fact of presenting native sexuality as violent.

The situation at the start of the play is one of frozen colonial stasis. The space of the island is synonymous with Prospero's control via the (magic) learning of the Old World. Suggestively, Prospero's powers derive from his books, brought from Milan—a source of knowledge by definition *transcendent* of the place itself.

Prospero's very dominance is created through a repression of the feminine and native magic of the isle. We are given very little sense of Caliban's hypnotic mother. Surely her imprisoning of Ariel in a tree could simply be a distorted reading of the way feminine or Earth Mother magic construes spirit as immanent in the (sacred) earth. Prospero has "freed" the spirit to what he regards is "proper" Sky Father separation from matter.

On the other hand, like modernity itself, Prospero cannot really let the spirit go. Knowledge goes hand in hand with power in modernity, as Jung well knew. So Prospero keeps the spirit as agent of his colonial power, which mimics the transcendent God by keeping hold of Ariel, a symbol of his knowledge-as-power over the conquered territory. Jung could see that the conquest of nature and of other lands are two halves of modernity's conversion of transcendence, from spiritual *looking up* to avaricious *looking out*. Prospero's actions incarnate the gaze that is greedy for knowledge/power.

As Shakespeare suggests in *The Tempest*, Prospero's lack of human connection in Milan, expressed by his looking *up* to magical spirits, gets him cast *out*. He then converts his learning into power over the land and its population. Ultimately, however, the play has him re-examine the mistakes he had made in Milan. For *The Tempest* is not just about colonialism. It is also about the future history of what happens when the colonialists go home.

At the beginning of the play, Prospero commands the elements. He makes a storm, and this time is the *agent* not *victim* of a shipwreck. His usurping brother, Alonzo, is washed up on the island along with his attendant lords. Divided from them, and believed dead, is Alonzo's son, Ferdinand, who is discovered by Miranda. Prospero manipulates the young people into falling in love through yet another demonstration of colonial capriciousness. Here of course it is an *act* for political purposes. Such a display of "acting" points to the play itself as participating in the genre of rule through *performance*. Tudor England *performed* the incarnation of power through processions, masques, and public executions. Such rule by performing energized the later spectacles of colonialism.

A third and final group of survivors are a cluster of sailors. They, appropriately enough, encounter Caliban, who enlists them into a revolt against Prospero. Meanwhile, Prospero starts to face the one power that really threatens his dominance: his own rage at his ill treatment at home. In the comically ludicrous revolt by the underclass sailors with the indigenous Caliban, we see the emergence of colonial and post-colonial political movements. These draw on divisions and inequalities in the conquering as well as conquered nations. The emergence of colonialism had *everything* to do with conflicts from which people were escaping, as both Prospero and the sailors demonstrate.

In order to go home, Prospero has to forgive. In order to truly forgive, he must become a man again and cease trying to imitate a god. He has to renounce transcendence through power, his privileged place separate and above, and accept the dialogical relation of transcendence and immanence, spirit and matter in human embodiment. As the play puts it, he has to stop controlling spirit for the sake of power. Ariel should be set free, to come only when he pleases and not when Prospero pleases. And Prospero has to accept what he has made of Caliban, of the island's native inhabitant. "This thing of darkness, I acknowledge mine," he says.[20]

Unpunished for his attempted revolution, Caliban has been brutalized by occupation and is at last left alone on the island. After colonialism is over, and all the Milanese have gone, Caliban is the Jungian sign of the post-colonial population. His culture has been stripped from him, he was cruelly "converted" from son (of Sycorax) to slave (of Prospero), and the spirit was taken away from the matter of the island. Yet, by virtue of what colonialism in the person of Prospero has done to Caliban, he is also *symbol* for the politics of Milan via the soul of Prospero. This "thing of darkness" belongs to the darkness of Old World power, and most crucially, *forms the darkness of the former colonial nations* as they sail away, leaving the terror of a denatured and dispirited culture behind. Caliban is a Jungian symbol for the unexplored darkness of power in European Milan.

The Tempest is a future history in which the island becomes a time-space structure for colonialism and its aftermath. The sea journey between Milan and the island is one of time also. It is worth noting that the play, perhaps through its deep spiritual treatment of power and learning, does provide optimistic glimpses that suggest a future as yet unknown in the twenty-first century. After all, Ferdinand and Miranda are not a story of power, but one of love.

As representative and heir of the Old World, Ferdinand is not allowed to have Miranda as a sexual conquest. In order to win her, he is forced to serve her father. He thus accepts the culture he finds on the island and learns to respect the woman he adores. And she proves, if anything, to be his superior (as daughter of the true duke) in the hierarchy of the Old World. Still, the relationship is forged across cultures and through Prospero's play-acting, in spite of the arbitrariness of transcendent power.

Moreover, Prospero's return can only be accomplished through his coming to terms with his own darkness, with the figure of Caliban and with his burning desire for revenge. To regain authentic power in Milan, he has to renounce the spiritually transcendent power he has set up on the island. He throws away his magician's staff and his books. The end of colonialism is the end of a certain sort of spiritual power.

The Tempest tells us that Western culture as a whole, and the individuals within it, have to go home by coming to terms with our own darkness. Going home (to Milan) is the space-time image of meaning which the play offers the modern audience. Going home may be a metaphorical journey into the Self.

Going home may take us back to Mother Nature and to an embrace of the sacred as being immanent as well as transcendent. Going home is to set Ariel free, the spirit that we have used and abused in the quest for transcendent power and knowledge. Going home almost certainly means letting go of much that has been grasped too fiercely. We must let go of Prospero's staff and his books. We have to let go our anxious need to grab logos. To do so is to seek for wholeness in the writing and re-writing of mythos.

Today in the aftermath of so much colonial history, we may share in Prospero's loneliness and in our own hope that Ariel may return.

Last Words

I have devoted a chapter to myth and history because Jung believed these to be entwined. For him, myth is the special kind of narrative that both represents and shapes the psyche, and knits us into the collective. Myths that weave the individual into the psychic life of the world do so by enlivening our collective consciousness of knowable matters with the energizing life of the partially unknowable collective unconscious. This collectivity through mythical narrative is history.

Jung also recognized that myth works in two ways: psychic narratives can generate abstract truths (logos) or they can be the source of immanent creativity and endless stories (mythos). Just as the individual needs a balance of both types of myth, so does a society. Indeed we need to recognize that both types of myth are mutually sustaining as well as differentiating. They are transcendent Sky Father and immanent Earth Mother in mutual embrace.

Modernity has sown the seeds of its own darkness in privileging Sky Father logos so far over Earth Mother mythos that "she" is as angry as her son, Caliban. So Jung's *treatment* of myth is an attempt to redeem history. For the individual patient, he tried in analysis to help them find those immanent myths of being in the stories of individuation.

In the dispute with Freud, Jung finds his own need to bring a compensatory emphasis on mythos and radical typology to the construction of a psychology. So foundational is this difference in emphasis that the process of mythos dialoguing with logos becomes integral to Jung's writing. Indeed, I am arguing finally that Jung's psychological writing is a compensatory myth for modern science. It is a myth generating a logos of conceptual, abstract truths, yet also and even more, and in order to keep privileging the creative, unknowable unconscious, it is generative of a radical typology mythos of psyche.

I looked at Shakespeare's *The Tempest* as an atypical work of history. Chosen for its visionary qualities (see Chapter 3), its mythical structure shows the return to humanity of the banished god/magician. Such a reading allows the future-oriented direction of the Jungian psyche to sponsor an imaginative history.

Such questions of history and myth in the work of Jung lead to others about his attitudes to modernity's key issues of science, religion, politics, gender, and power. These will form the matter of the next two chapters. In the final chapter, we will look at how Jung anticipates some of the most far-reaching shifts indicated in the twenty-first century, those suggesting a new holistic paradigm. Such profound changes include a transformation of relationships to technology, nature, cultural theory, and even consciousness itself. Did Jung prophesy the death of the Western ego? Or its rebirth?

FURTHER READING

Michael Vannoy Adams, *The Mythological Unconscious* (New York and London: Karnac, 2001).
Here Adams develops Jung's argument on the collective unconscious in order to demonstrate the mythical quality of the contemporary world.

Joseph Campbell, *The Hero with a Thousand Faces* (Princeton: Princeton University Press, 1968).
Hugely influential and still out there influencing Hollywood block-busters, Campbell explores the heroic forms of masculinity in world myth.

Laurence Coupe, *Myth* (London and New York: Routledge, 1997).
An introduction to myth that is as lively in its form as in its subject matter. Comprehensive and yet focused, Coupe's work is superb.

Seamus Heaney, *Opened Ground* (London: Faber & Faber, 1998).
Heaney has allied himself with Jung's view of the unconscious.

Lucy Huskinson, ed., *Dreaming the Myth Onwards: New Directions in Jungian Therapy and Thought* (London and New York: Routledge, 2008).
A diverse and provocative essay collection from an international range of scholars. It takes Jung's ideas about myth and history forward into the new century.

Robert A. Segal, ed., *Jung on Mythology* (London and New York: Routledge, 1998).
All of Jung's important passages on myth, selected and introduced by eminent myth scholar, Robert A. Segal.

Robert A. Segal, *Myth: A Very Short Introduction* (Oxford: Oxford University Press, 2004).
Pithy and packed, this is an excellent starting point for the study of myth.

William Shakespeare, *The Tempest* (London: The Arden Shakespeare, 2000).

Dennis Slattery and Glen Slater, eds., *Varieties of Mythic Experience: Essays on Religion, Psyche and Culture* (Switzerland: Daimon Verlag, 2008).
An essay collection by first rank scholars making important contributions to the study of myth as psychology, literature, and tragedy, and of the way myth structures relations between the human and the non-human.

Salley Vickers, *Where Three Roads Meet* (Edinburgh: Canongate, 2007).
This enjoyable and imaginative re-telling of the myth of Oedipus has the figure of Tiresias visiting Sigmund Freud in London as he approaches death. It is a wonderful exploration of the different treatment of myth by Jung and Freud. In a sense, this small novel brings them all to the same place where three roads meet.

Jung and Science, Alchemy, and Religion

Dreams and Visions

Jung always insisted on the significance of the personal factor in his ideas. The psyche contains an unknowable alien force in the unconscious; inevitably, the doctor, scientist, or theorist will need to draw on what is *personal to him/her* in approaching this force. The importance of Jung's own dreams and visions to his life and work are testament to the importance he placed on his individual psychic experiences.

For example, in *Memories, Dreams, Reflections* (*MDR*), Jung portrays himself as a sensitive, unfocused youth torn between studying the sciences and the humanities.[1] He has two dreams that he interprets at the time as directing him toward the sciences. In one, he appears as an archaeologist, this being one of his passions. He digs into burial mounds and discovers the bones of prehistoric monsters, and immediately feels gripped by the idea of penetrating the secrets of nature. Jung's second dream presents the mysteries of nature in iridescent living form. He is wandering in a dark wood with streams threading through it, when he comes upon a circular pool dominated by a huge glistening jellyfish. (Much later, in the 1950s, Jung used this very dream of a round fish to indicate a living mandala form: the pulsating image of the living Self in the unconscious.²) Jung's musings eventually took him into medicine. The natural settings in these dreams, however, illustrate the way unconscious material points to the unknown and refuses to respect disciplinary boundaries. Nature here conveys an overwhelming sense of awe and implicit far-reaching significance that could not be rationally defined and therefore not "confined" to one sphere of knowledge. In truth, Jung's dreams and visions in his early life refuse to respect the conventions of his proper Swiss boyhood.

One of the most famous episodes in *MDR* finds the young Jung pondering God when he suddenly begins to feel oppressed by intimations of some horrible sin he is certain he will commit, if he allows his mind to go where it wants to go.³ But the boy decides that, since an all-powerful God must have *intended* Adam and Eve to disobey, God must be willing his own sinfulness! So he allows the forbidden image to form in his mind. He finds himself visualizing a beautiful cathedral in a sparkling blue sky, when all at once, God lets fall an enormous turd from above and shatters the dome!

Feeling as though he has *allowed* this image to be channeled through his psyche, the young boy feels at once a sensation of peace and of having experienced the paradoxical will of God. Later, Jung will come to define this kind of experience as *both* the will of God *and* the autonomous activity of the unconscious. For the unconscious speaks in dreams, images, and visions, and its creativity, unknowability, and sublimity are those very qualities that in another age, in another language, have been called God.

Where God is symbolized as a numinous, unfathomable depth of significance, there the psyche is to be found. Indeed, Jung the therapist is very happy for these unconscious powers to be called God, providing those using the language do so out of a living connection with these words. Religion ought to provide a living symbolism to regulate our relationship to the unconscious, according to Jung. Where that has ceased to be—as in a secular modernity characterized either by unbelief or by a defensive, stagnant sort of belief whose words have lost their symbolic connections to the psyche—then the historical moment calls for another script for inner being.

The turd smashing the cathedral has much to teach us because it is a marvelous visual encapsulation of Jung's attitude to religion throughout his career. Firstly, it is a visualization and not a doctrine or a creed. Consequently, its meaning cannot easily be explained in words, nor limited to what words can say. The image strongly partakes of the mystery and unknowability of the unconscious psyche. Secondly, it is a violent assault on respectably organized religion, and in particular upon the social arts (for example, cathedral building) mobilized to contain the religious impulse.

God, in Jung's vision, brutally desecrates a complex work of collective consciousness designed to house Him. Just so will the unconscious psyche rise up in ungovernable violence, flooding individual and collective consciousness, if aspects of it are too long denied. For Jung believes that God shits on His cathedral if we forget His dark side. The child Jung has realized God's cruelty to Adam and Eve: God intended them to sin, and then punished them for it. The much older Jung will become pre-occupied with the problems of Job, a pious Old Testament man treated viciously by God in order to test his fidelity.

God, Jung writes throughout his life, is not only a source of the good. God has a dark side. Deny this dark side of God and you cut yourself and your culture off from the reality of the psyche. God, dark and light, is the name we have traditionally given to the source of our being in the partly unknowable and creative unconscious. To refer back to Jung's dreams from before he chose a career in science, we might say that investigating nature will become for him an investigation into the "place" where *human becomes nature*: the unconscious.

Dreams and visions are the direct expression of human nature. They are also communications from "God," because religion is another language for speaking about the same material. To Jung, psychology—psyche-logos, the logos *of* psyche—is science *and* religion. It is thus not surprising that he became fascinated by ancient alchemy, a cultural practice in which science and religion were explicitly connected.

This chapter will look further at the nature of Jung's science and of the importance of alchemy to his work. It will include his attempts to offer a new principle of science with the sort of "meaningful coincidences" he dubbed *synchronicity*. And I will show how he sought, through these developments, to change modernity. Jung was interested in a science of symbols and felt that alchemy was a possible historical source, along with myth. With such a science, he believed that he could re-orient the modern psyche so that it could become "at home" in the world it has created.

Was Jung a Scientist?

As a young doctor working in a mental hospital, Jung treated a woman who believed she lived on the moon.[4] The moon was beautiful but its inhabitants were afflicted by a terrible vampire who preyed on the women and children. One day the woman decided to kill the vampire, and she approached him with a knife. The vampire opened his wings, revealing himself as a ravishingly handsome young man. He enfolded the woman in his embrace and flew off with her. Jung opposed this vampire lover; as her doctor, he was to keep her connected to the earth. But to her this lower domain was not beautiful, and she was deeply unhappy here.

Eventually, through talking to Jung, she came to accept life on Earth. She was discharged from the hospital and treated in the community. Of this incident, Jung says that he learned the importance of listening carefully to fantasy in seriously disturbed patients. His therapeutic approach was to work with the unconscious visionary world of the patient, until its effect on her whole life could be made bearable. Paradoxically, he had to *engage with* the fantasy realm, acknowledging its genuine power, for by agreeing with the patient that visions from the unconscious are "real"—in the sense of having lasting meaning, importance, and value—Jung could begin to reconcile her to everyday existence. In this way, the patient's own experiences of the Other were validated, while she could be encouraged to accept the limitations of life "grounded" in the ego.

Here is Jung the pragmatist and healer. While, on the one hand, his whole project is aimed at revaluing the emissaries from the unconscious for Western modernity, for some vulnerable patients, the unconscious has become "too real." Jung did not believe that the modern person should decamp to the unconscious! Rather, he thought that everyone needed to structure a creative relationship with the unconscious in the process known as "individuation." Patients ended up in mental hospitals when the powers of the unconscious swallowed them up; these people needed help to begin a conscious differentiation from "demons." Those patients who arrived at Jung's consulting room tended to be at once haunted by these "demons" and starved of contact with the unconscious. This different kind of suffering required initiation into the unconscious underworld of dreams. Above all, Jung's work aimed at "balance," at the achievement of a healthy dialogue between ego and unconscious. For the modern Western world, that meant a rebalancing of the creation myths.

Three principal figures are behind what the modern world casually calls "science" (by which we are referring to the modern paradigm of materialist science): Francis Bacon (1561-1626),[5] René Descartes (1596-1650),[6] and Isaac Newton (1642-1727).[7] From Bacon comes the paramount importance of scientific method as a means of determining truth. In *Novum Organum*,[8] he described the scientific method that is still cited today, which consists of collecting reliable data, then classifying and generalizing it. Such a procedure is prelude to conducting experiments with the data in order to structure a hypothesis or theory. Scientific theory is then "proved" by repeating the experiment. Scientific "truth" is only attained through repeated results. Reality is thus considered "fixed" and reliable, the product of universal laws.

Descartes provides some philosophical underpinning for this assumption of a rule-governed universe. In *Discourse on Method*, he rejected the prevailing Aristotelian idea of *teleology*: that everything in nature had purpose, emotion, and intelligence.[9] Rather, he saw nature as inanimate and governed by a series of physical laws. Moreover, Descartes intensified the dualism of Western philosophy by asserting that the mind was separate from the body and humans separate from nature. He drew attention to the quality of rational intelligence as characteristic of the human, as distinct from nature. And, of course, reason was regarded as innately masculine, as it had been before the work of Descartes.

Isaac Newton became the major proponent of Enlightenment views of the scientific universe. So influential was he that this scientific paradigm did not begin to be challenged until the emergence of sub-atomic physics and Einstein's work in the early twentieth century. Crucially, despite Newton's own continuing interest in 3 (see later in this chapter), he and many others had dispensed with any idea of the universe as alive in itself. The natural world could be wholly understood as obeying fixed laws. In time, this became the belief that knowledge of these laws would enable *everything* to be known.

Newton advocated the principle of *reductionism*, which not only argued that the world could be reduced to a series of laws, but that reducing everything to the smallest unit and studying that could lead to an understanding of the whole. Hence the importance of studying what he thought was the smallest unit of reality, the atom. Answer the puzzles of the atom and theories could be scaled up to explain the whole universe. Yet reductionism also means dividing up knowledge into different disciplines, on the assumption that such separate, specialist knowledge alone will get to the heart of the matter.

Newton believed in studying reality mathematically. He formulated three laws of motion and one of gravitation in *Philosophiae Naturalis Principia Mathematica*.[10] He also provided us with the famous metaphor of the universe as a clock, set going by God and then simply, mechanically proceeding. In the atomistic Newtonian world view, with reality made up of discrete unchanging objects in an empty space, time moves in a uniform and unidirectional way. Thus events were related causally, like billiard balls. Scientists began to treat the world more and more as an object, "out there;" "objectivity" became the great scientific criterion. Indeed, the recognition of "out there" leads to the notion of the "Other," which comes with the separation of subject and object. Also characteristic of Newtonian science is the belief that the world is infinitely knowable, because separate from the observer, who can look upon it "objectively."

These ways of constructing knowledge are still regarded as "scientific" in the twenty-first century. This is despite the fact that, even as far back as Bacon, many called for the imagination to be given a place in the framework of "science." In addition, from the beginning of the twentieth century, the Newtonian paradigm began to be challenged by quantum and relativity theory. Chapter 7 will look at the new sciences of emergence and complexity. For this chapter we need to note the two major challenges to the Newtonian perspective in Jung's lifetime. Einstein's relativity challenged reductionism by showing that reality was far more like an inter-dependent fabric than discrete and atomistic. Everything really is connected to everything else! Second, quantum experiments showed that the observer is always implicated in what is observed; there is no absolute scientific objectivity. Hence there is no absolute subject/object division. We are not wholly divided from the nature that we gaze upon.

It is evident from these examples that "science" is a contested term that has developed over centuries of endeavor. In modernity, "science" comes to be used both precisely and loosely. Precisely, it stands for adherence to Newtonian and Baconian principles of method, laws, and objectivity. Loosely, science comes to indicate knowledge that is regarded as more "important" or more "true" than other types of knowledge, such as those secured through the arts or humanities.

Indeed, Jung uses the term "science" to indicate "rational and conceptual knowledge," that which can be deduced and written about. He says, however, that the rational knowledge gained from *breaking life down* into discrete elements is itself secondary to the *living mystery* of the psyche.[11] For him, the Newtonian practice of reductionism produces knowledge of a decidedly secondary reality.

On the other hand, Jung claims to be a scientist because of his Baconian attitude to the data about the unconscious he has collected from the dream images of his patients, upon which he bases his hypotheses. He claims to be a scientist theorizing from evidence. Yet there is a problem in appealing to Baconian and Newtonian approaches when the data is from the unconscious. First, where is objectivity when the *object* of study, the psyche, is also the *means* of study, the psyche of the scientist? This applies whether scrutinizing one's own psychic images or those of another.

In fact, Jung's therapeutic practice is the complete antithesis of scientific objectivity, as is all psychoanalysis. Rather than try to bracket out or bypass the person of the doctor, psychoanalysis relies upon the agitation of the unconscious psyches of both the patient *and* the therapist to create a *healing connection* between the two. In order to account for this phenomenon, Freud had introduced the notion of *transference*, to signify that the patient transfers part of their unconscious matter onto their image of the analyst. Jung, however, was the first to grasp the importance of the analyst's reciprocal *counter-transference*. He suggested that the analyst should regard his or her own unconscious reactions as valuable communication from the unconscious of the patient itself, as yet unavailable to the conscious mind. Freudian and Jungian analysis is a "science" of connection. It directly challenges the Newtonian principle of privileging objectivity, as well as the Cartesian insistence upon the necessity of a subject/object division.

It is nevertheless important at this point to note that Jung adhered largely to Descartes' subject/object division in the *terminology* by which he expressed his ideas. For example, opposing a conscious ego to an unconscious that is in part unknowable, he typically refers to this unconscious as "objective." By this he means that the unconscious is autonomous, that it is not limited to, nor does it derive from, the ego. The goal of individuation is to overcome the cultural dualism that separates consciousness from its natural *connection* with the unconscious, and thus to experience a union, a wholeness.

Jung saw his work as adhering to aspects of the Newtonian paradigm, but also as related to the new science of relativity. In "On the Nature of the Psyche," he sets out his attitudes to psychic knowledge.[12] The essay moves from deductions about the existence and implications of the unconscious, to establishing the historical tradition of working with the unconscious in alchemy. It then offers some radical evocations of what a "science of the unconscious" might mean, especially in the context of the nuclear age.

Jung and Science: "On the Nature of the Psyche"

This important essay in Jung's *Collected Works* illustrates the challenges and the consequences of Jung's fundamental attitude to knowledge. This is, of course, based upon the creative, in part unknowable unconscious as a *source*, a founding absent/presence that affects everything.[13] How is it possible to be a scientist in the Baconian-Newtonian sense when working with the unknowable? After all, Newton believed that an understanding of cosmic laws and a reductionist approach would gradually reveal all mysteries. Bacon insisted upon the repeatability of scientific experiments—a difficulty when the data consists of dreams!

The issue, in part, comes down to the varieties of argument used. Argument is roughly divided into two traditions, logic and rhetoric. Like other dualist divisions described in this book, logic and rhetoric are by no means mutually exclusive. No argument can stick entirely to one method or the other. Logical exposition still needs the metaphors and persuasive qualities of language. In turn, rhetoric must base some of its emotional force on reason and deduction. As well as these different traditions of argument, there are also different varieties within them. Conceptual argument is based upon unfolding and exploring the implications of a logical concept; it does not draw upon external data from the world. Jung uses a great deal of conceptual argumentation in "On the Nature of the Psyche" in trying to elucidate the concepts of "consciousness" and "unconsciousness."

The other type of argument is, of course, empirical, which draws upon the reading of data. Bacon's scientific method is a rational organizing of empirical data, gained from experiments. With the later division of knowledge into academic disciplines and the expansion of the scientific ideal to almost all disciplines, the exact nature of this "data" changes according to which discipline is employed. For instance, when working as a literary scholar, my data will be literary texts. A historian may use many varieties of data, from archaeological remains, contemporary artifacts, and documents, to other historians' books. Psychology, a relatively new discipline, continually tests the assumptions of what might be appropriate data for theorizing. Even today, many psychologists stick to experiments recognizable to Bacon.

However, both Freud and Jung, pioneers of psychoanalysis, expanded the range of material incorporated into their work as data. Freud used literature, archaeology, visual art, philosophy, as well as reported material from patients. "On the Nature of the Psyche" embeds data drawn from other psychologists, philosophy, physics, and alchemy in a largely rhetorical argument designed to *draw the reader into* the model of the psyche as a living, numinous mystery. Ultimately, Jung's scientific argument is not *about* the psyche; it is a creative act that incorporates the reader. As such, it marks a movement of "science" from the Newtonian paradigm to a new framework for the twenty-first century, holism (see Chapter 7).

The Wheel, the Web, and the Tail-Eating Serpent

One way of looking at the rhetorical structuring of Jung's scientific writing in "On the Nature of the Psyche" is to see it as *incorporating the reader in a ritual.* The essay does this by means of its circular structure, which "seeds" ideas and then returns to them again and again until they have flowered into potent poetic life. Two examples are Jung's notion of *archetypes* and his variations on the metaphor of *light.*

The word "archetype" is used early on in the essay as if it were already an established psychological notion, but the full development of the concepts of consciousness and the unconscious that constitute the basic evidence for archetypes comes only many paragraphs later. Even more striking is the development of the image of light and darkness. It begins as a dim intuition, that there is more to the psyche than ego, expressed metaphorically as a faint ray signifying new knowledge. The metaphor is then extended and the light spectrum—from violet to infra-red—used to illustrate the polar structure of the psyche, between instinct on the former and spirit on the latter end. Finally, it builds to evoking the beautiful image found in alchemy of *multiple luminosities*, of many points of light clustering in the dark sky. By this point in the discussion, light has become more than metaphor: it is now a *symbol*, used by Jung (echoing alchemy) to evoke the multiple *qualities* of the unconscious, while also suggesting that multiple points of light correspond to the *actuality* of archetypes in the unconscious. Often, in rhetoric, both the content (meaning) and the figure representing the content (form) themselves become two sorts of perspective on the same idea. Thus, archetypes are *like* stars, and our understanding of the firmament, our light of knowledge is also a psychological *truth*. Ultimately, this rhetorical strategy and the affective energy of the language propel the argument.

The ritual quality of "On the Nature of the Psyche" works by more than repetition. Ritual is enacted in the dialogical structure of the argument itself. Jung's writing persona depends upon an answering response from the reader; the argument is open-ended. Instead of a rational highway to a known destination, it is a voyage of discovery for reader and author alike. Early on, this open-endedness is expressed by the competitive citation of earlier psychologists and philosophers, arranged to show that something remains wanting in their efforts: the quest must go on. Citation also sets up a historical dimension to Jung's psychology. Past errors give way to a truer present, although present ideas are not yet fully revealed.

In this way the historical argument of scientific progress is firmly problematized *before* Jung discloses his actual position: that he, Jung, cannot accept what is implicit in the Newtonian-Baconian paradigm, a narrative of wholly rational, linear scientific progress. Rather, Jung de-centers this narrative of a dominating science just as he de-centers the dominating ego he characterizes as its product. This is a vital point about Jung's writing: the *argument* of "On the Nature of the Psyche" unites with his mainly rhetorical *methods* of writing. Effectively, Jung uses the rhetorical arts not just to describe his psychology, but to enact it. "On the Nature of the Psyche" is an act of science as well as an act of literary creation.

The main way that Jung de-centers linear scientific progress is by introducing alchemy. Though a historical phenomenon, alchemy is not dead and gone. The historical timeline, according to Jung, will loop back. Here is another example of the developing repetition that is found throughout the essay. The argument becomes a web of inter-connections rather than a logical progression.

In such a way, "On the Nature of the Psyche" faithfully *performs* Jung's key notion of prioritizing what is creative and partly unknowable. Jung calls his final vision a "net of reflections," in which psychology itself is only part of a web spanning all kinds of knowledge.[14] He was also particularly drawn to the image of the uroboros, the tail-eating serpent from alchemy, as embodying the self-fertilizing, self-devouring psyche. Jung's reader is "in-corporated" into the living processes of his vision, inside the uroboros-like essay.

Jung and Alchemy

What particularly excited Jung about alchemy? After all, the practice was generally considered the mere historical precursor to chemistry, science still hampered by its enmeshment with religion, according to Enlightenment followers of the Newtonian paradigm. (Ironically, this did not include Newton himself, who took alchemy very seriously. In working through Renaissance alchemy texts, Jung has an illustrious predecessor.)

Alchemy is documented from the first century c.e. in Islamic texts, and claims for its lineage go back to Ancient Egypt. Alchemists believed that matter and spirit were not separate, as Christian theology taught. Whereas Christian teaching placed a patriarchal God above the material world, alchemists saw the divine in nature. Alchemy is here an inheritance of the Earth Mother creation myth of a sacred generative Earth. However, by the time of the Renaissance texts that Jung used, alchemists had been sufficiently influenced by Christianity to believe that God needed to be rescued from matter. It was the task of the alchemist, by study and by working with matter in his laboratory, to extract the divine spirit.

The base matter of lead could become the high spiritual matter of gold, as well as the divine "water of life" or the "Philosopher's Stone" that bestowed immortality. Alchemy inevitably attracted not only the serious, but also those who merely wanted to make gold or to cheat others by claiming they had done so. But despite the resulting public relations problem, alchemy became a highly complex practice combining practical experiment, philosophy, religious belief, and creative art, producing texts full of the most esoteric symbols. And the alchemists did make important chemical discoveries. Yet after Newton, a split occurred between the artistic, philosophical side of alchemy and the work on matter in the laboratory. The numinous and imaginative aspects were stripped away to leave a material-based scientific practice: modern chemistry.

Jung was fascinated by alchemy's premise of inspirited matter, and his book, *Psychology and Alchemy*, is his most sustained treatment of the meaning of the ongoing mystery of alchemy for his psychology.[15] He viewed alchemists as having had a different relationship with God than orthodox Christians. Whereas the Church preached that God above was separate and perfect, the alchemists were *aiding* God in the work of Creation by helping the divine spirit escape from dark matter.[16]

Alchemy develops a *partnership* with the divine that significantly resembles Jung's emphasis on the connection to the unconscious. Recall that to Jung, religious experience is authentic experience of the unconscious, whether or not one believes in a god. Remember as well his idea that working productively with the unconscious (that is, individuation) is aiding God in his on-going creation of consciousness.

Jung, in fact, holds *two* attitudes to alchemy, one emerging from the Newtonian paradigm and the other from the new holistic science. When thinking from the Cartesian position of the absolute subject/object division, Jung believed the alchemists were *projecting* their psyches onto matter, that in working with chemicals in their laboratories, they were actually operating on their own unconscious.[17] Alchemists were engaged in an individuation process, while believing they were rescuing divine spirit from base matter.

However, Jung is inevitably drawn beyond the limitations of this notion of projection, with its home in the subject/object division. Here Jung's writing anticipates both ecocritical and ecophilosophical attempts to reposition the human in a continuum with nature. Jung finds in alchemy the evocation of an *ecology* of the human psyche. To alchemy, the imagination finds substance in nature and super-nature alike. So birds are thoughts, along with other winged creatures from the imagination such as angels and the rather devilish alchemical figure of Mercurius.[18] Just as the phoenix, the vulture, and the raven represent the spiritual matter in its earlier, rougher stages, so the final *lapis* or Philosopher's Stone is sometimes given wings, signifying its ethereal properties.[19]

Unsurprisingly, alchemy texts in Christian cultures frequently invoke Christ. Crucially, though, alchemy does so from *within nature*, as well as by associating the final emancipated spirit with the resurrected god. A common alchemical image is the green lion, signifying a *natural* Christ whose color links him to both deathly putrefaction and the green rebirth in spring. "He" may also be analogous with "She," the divine virgin who is also, alchemically, a higher form of Mercurius.[20]

Rather than see this co-mingling as confusion, it is important to recognize it as a vision of nature radically outside the subject/object perspective. Nature is here a fluid dynamic process of inseparable natural and spiritual transformations. The human soul lives in this transformational space, as does the divine spirit. Alchemy is a material, philosophical, creative practice of *refining* divine spirit from its entanglement in base matter. Jung similarly had devised "individuation," in which the spiritual qualities of the Self were to be refined from the dark matter of less elevated psychic material. Yet alchemy adhered to a holistic view of reality where matter, spirit, and human soul exist as inter-related, and this perspective helped Jung construe the psyche in a new way.

It was when Jung made the connection between alchemical perspectives and the new science of relativity that he was forced to recognize—and came to partially adopt—the alchemical view of the world as an interconnected web. For alchemy, he notes, not only are mind and matter connected, but also *mind works on matter*. The imagination is a dynamic and material force that forms "subtle bodies," elements in a third realm between matter and spirit.[21] This intermediate realm of subtle reality is psychic, and, Jung says, his psychology and modern quantum physics are nearing this understanding today.[22] The notion of "subtle reality" leads us to Jung's great idea of his later years, synchronicity.

Synchronicity: God(dess) and Science

It is useful to look at Jung's notion of synchronicity in two ways. Firstly, it is his most overt attempt at a scientific description that fulfils his fundamental attitude to reality. Secondly, as Roderick Main has shown most persuasively, it is Jung's sustained attempt to reconcile religion and science.[23] Can Jung put God back into the mechanical "clockwork" universe?

Put simply, synchronicity is *meaningful coincidence*. The Newtonian paradigm assumes a mechanical universe in which time moves in a straight line and events happen due to cause and effect. Happenings that appear significant, yet for which we can find no causal mechanism, we ascribe to "mere coincidence." Yet this could be regarded as merely a Western prejudice. As Jung wrote in "Archaic Man," published in *Modern Man in Search of a Soul* in 1933, other cultures believe in omens and portents and *these beliefs seem to work for them* (see Chapter 2).[24] So Jung coined the term "synchronicity" to stand for those events where space-time relations appear more complex. Specifically, synchronicity indicates a meaningful rather than a causal connection between psyche and apparently material events.

Examples of synchronicity are often drawn from dreams: a dream appears to predict an event, which then occurs; a dream points to something simultaneously happening somewhere else, and not known to the dreamer until afterwards; a dream might be a spur to discovering something about the past. Dreams are not a *necessary* element of a synchronistic connection, but such a connection is by definition between a psychic and a material event.

Jung gave an example of a difficult woman patient who was unwilling to grant any value to the unconscious.[25] She was telling him of a dream in which she was given a golden scarab, when there was a knocking at the window. Jung opened it and caught a scarab-type beetle, which he recognized as an insect sacred to certain cultures. He gave the beetle to the

woman, suggesting that it was an indication her dream image had materialized in life. Apparently, this incident profoundly touched the woman,
and she began to trust in the reality and value of the creative psyche.

As a teacher, I have often discussed synchronicity with students. Many
claim to have had dreams that proved significant in terms that fit the
synchronistic model. For Jung, synchronicity was a way to augment the
Newtonian account of reality, specifically to deny the absoluteness of the
subject/object division. In synchronistic events, we are part of what we
observe. Moreover, we change what we observe by the act of observing it.

Synchronicity is furthermore Jung's contribution to the alchemical
vision of the world as a web of commingled matter, psyche, and spirit. It
is alchemical because, in becoming conscious of unconscious and potentially meaningful connections, we are participating in God's ongoing creation. Synchronicity is an attempt to bring God back into the Newtonian mechanical cause-and-effect universe, a divine principle of creation
through making meaning. The Newtonian universe has been *created*; the
synchronistic one is *creating and being created*.

This is yet another way of looking at individuation as realizing the
Self, which here means: to realize, to make real, to make conscious part
of God's numinous being as consciousness. Synchronicity is a vision of
God as hidden in the unconscious fabric of the universe, needing man to
aid in becoming conscious. In synchronicity, the understanding of these
meaningfully—rather than causally—connected events, is a contribution to the greater reality (realization of) God.

A last note about synchronicity looks forward to the next chapter on
gender, for it is in discussing this subject that Jung characterizes nature as
feminine. Typical Baconian scientific experiments, he says, force nature
to answer limited questions. What is needed is an approach that allows
nature to answer out of *her* wholeness.[26]

Of course, there is nothing new in regarding nature as feminine.
What is interesting is the concealed drama of synchronicity, the desire
on Jung's part to keep a connection with Christianity in his work. After
all, alchemists were far from orthodox in regarding matter as inspirited;
yet to their society they justified themselves by describing their work as
enabling the divine to attain a proper Christian transcendence of matter. Jung follows the Christian alchemical tradition in calling his pri-

mary image of the Self a "Christ" or "God image." In finding God in the matter of the psyche, Jung constructs a psychological model of worship of the risen (out of psyche) God.

Thus, in synchronicity, what is actually going on is a rescue of the masculine transcendent God from feminine matter. The rescue occurs by the act of understanding, of making the meaningful connection. That very formation of conscious meaning is the bringing of the divine spark of the Son out of the dark matter of the Mother. *Psychological theory mimics divine creation myth; or, creation myth is realized again in psychological narrative.*

Is this just another imposition of patriarchy by means of an account of reality, where patriarchy means the assumption that the primary creator and source of being is masculine, relegating all that is Other and secondary to the feminine? I would like to suggest that there is something more going on here.

It is important to note that Jung's feminine characterization of nature, although significantly occluded (see Chapter 6), is potentially revolutionary. Newtonian science assumes that the creator set the universe going, then stood back and allowed it to run like clockwork under universal laws. Essentially, Newton's is a reading of Genesis that stresses the godhead as working from a principle of separation; the greatest subject/object division is between God and universe. Such is not the vision of either alchemy or synchronicity.

Synchronicity relies upon the meaning-making capacity of archetypes. Archetypes are not the causal origins of synchronistic events; rather, they are factors structuring their meaning. Synchronistic events are *"acts of creation in time."*[27]

Synchronicity is a productive working together of the feminine (nature, dreams, and so on) and the masculine (the impulse toward consciousness and transcendence). Both feminine nature (in which nature is at once cosmos and psyche) and masculine meaning-making are active creative partners. "Acts of creation in time" indicate that synchronicity exceeds both the Newtonian paradigm and those who argue that a transcendent Sky Father god exists alone; on the contrary, "He" does not.

Just as the Jungian unconscious is androgynous, capable of producing feminine as well as masculine images, so is reality an on-going creation, with processes we have chosen to define as rational and masculine, as well as those of a feminine and creative nature. In Chapter 6, we will look at Jung's struggle with gender symbolism, modernity, and the psyche, where I will show how Jung is working with deeply gendered creation myths to provide a science of symbols. For now, I would emphasize synchronicity as Jung's contribution to a new holistic paradigm of science, one that places humanity *within* complex processes of creation.

A Science of Symbols

Jung's mythical scheme of the two types of creation myth was discussed in Chapter 3. Now we have seen that Newtonian science owes its origins to the Sky Father myth of *separation*, while synchronicity is a manifestation of Earth Mother as the creative principle connecting psyche, body, soul, spirit, and nature. To bring these two gendered myths of consciousness together, Jung, in his treatment of religion, his alchemical theories, and his therapy of dreams, offers the *symbol*.

Recall Jung's distinction between signs and symbols, outlined in the essay on poetry: signs represent a known or knowable entity, whereas symbols remain, at least in part, mysterious, for they indicate something not yet known or unknowable.[28] In pointing to the unknown, symbols are imbued with the energy of the unconscious; they also follow the patterns of archetypal images. Ultimately, Jung's notion of symbols is an attempt to expand science beyond the Newtonian paradigm. Their mystery is *conceptually protected* from scientific reductionism and the model of the mechanical universe.

The symbol is the union of psyche, body, and matter.[29] Indeed, only the symbol can express this shift from dualism to holism, the overcoming of subject/object division.

> The symbol is neither abstract nor concrete, neither rational, nor irrational, neither real nor unreal. It is always both ...[30]

Jung in his alchemy writings allowed himself to be drawn into the alchemical world of inspirited matter and human psyche in continuum. In alchemy, Jung finds a grammar of symbols that does not confine soul to the body as *interior*, but rather undoes the separation between inside and outside. Alchemists referred to this vision of human body and imagination indivisible from nature as the "subtle body": mind, body, and world co-creating, while the supposedly fixed boundaries between them are revealed as cultural, rather than actual. Indeed, here is another crucial property of symbols: they are cultural and historical. Not reducible to either culture or history—since the symbol itself works against reduction of any kind, and must, to remain symbolic, retain the prime mystery of the unknowable unconscious—yet symbols are necessarily embodied, and inherently part of the fabric of social reality. After all, if symbols unite the individual with the world, they do so through social patterns of meaning and discourse. Symbols are processes of psychic creation, operating between individuals and the narratives of their socio-cultural world.

Found in speculative, poetic, and imaginal systems of meaning such as religion, the arts, and mythical texts like those of alchemy, symbols problematize the division between representation and reality. Thus Jung's attitude to knowledge, given the key role he ascribes to symbols, necessarily refuses materialism. He describes materialism as merely another variety of unfounded adherence to a single principle of meaning, with no proven basis. Materialism is modernity's version of the "One God."

For Jung, reality could never be absorbed by social discourses, as some other critical theories maintain. On the other hand, he does not deny that human life is lived through images and narratives of particular cultures. The crucial distinction he makes is that the most deeply self-creating images and narratives will have an-Other dimension. They will symbolically weave the psyche *through* culture and *into* nature—the nature of the deep collective psyche and the fabric of the cosmos.

Social discourses tend to be made up of signs rather than symbols, structuring knowable social ideas. Signs are not enough to sustain a social system, however, because they cannot *incarnate* the psyches and selves of the populace. So a culture needs symbols, in the Jungian sense of the word, in at least some of its powerful narratives. Indeed, a powerful cultural narrative imbued with symbols is a *myth*, precisely because of its potent psychic creativity.

Symbols are responsible for the dynamism of myths. A narrative with symbols is a myth, just as an image with mythical properties becomes a symbol. The symbol is thus a node of creation, the fruit of the union of Sky Father and Earth Mother, uniting to sponsor both necessary types of consciousness, rational discrimination as well as loving connectedness.

Therefore symbols not only unite the psyche to its particular culture; they also unite the culture to nature. A symbol is a speck of embodied space-time. In the creative union of space and time in the symbol, culture and nature themselves can no longer be distinguished.

Jung thought that alchemy supplied invaluable sources of luminous symbols. He believed that the culture of the modern world was sick because it had gone too far in rejecting the numinosity of symbols. So he tried to do something about it.

The Science of Saving the World

To Jung, religions ought to be the prime source of symbols knitting together the individual psyche and society. This is no longer the case for the Western citizen. Modern Christianity has dwindled into a set of rules and impossible beliefs, impossible because the churches no longer possess the living symbols that could give people access to the mysterious power of the unconscious. As a result, Jung devoted much later writing to trying to re-invigorate Christian symbols. One fascinating example is his *Answer to Job*,[31] essentially a lively, comical re-writing of the Bible. Upright patriarch, Job was tormented by God, who wanted to test his faithfulness. Eventually, having lost everything, Job cries out against his unfair treatment. He had done everything God wanted, so why this cruelty?

Jung thought that Job was insufficiently answered by God's relenting. Like other commentators, he considered the incarnation of Christ a direct reply to Job. The pain of the Divine Son on the Cross answers, in some way, the pain of human beings. Yet what is important about Jung's biography of God is the way the story illustrates two key ideas. First of all, Jung's God is capable of terror and destruction as well as goodness and creation. Moreover, this dual nature of good and evil is a problem—for God, like man, wants to become conscious. The second idea in *Answer to Job* is the role of creative writing in healing, which I will come to below.

If man does not help God to become more conscious, then God (the collective unconscious) will spill its growing darkness into the modern world. Man helps God to become conscious by individuating himself. By increasing our own consciousness through coming to terms with the darkness of the collective unconscious, we become another spark of consciousness for/in the godhead.

Modernity's blindness is to ignore God/the unconscious, the powerful Other within. This inflates the unconscious until the wrath of unindividuated energy is let loose. Indeed, we have allowed the darkness of God/ collective unconsciousness to become incarnated in terrible weapons of mass destruction. In a world where materialism is the creed, matter itself is God. Nuclear, chemical, and biological weapons are the wrath of a God whom we have failed to contain in our symbolism. *Answer to Job* is an attempt to infuse narrative and its images with enough strength, vitality, and numinosity to become mythic, symbolic. We need a new myth and new symbols to contain the apocalyptic power of modern warfare.[32]

The four sinister horsemen ... are still waiting; already the atom bomb hangs over us ... [33]

The Bible ends with Apocalypse in the Book of Revelation; Christianity as a myth concludes with a terrible annihilation. Jung shows how this myth has found material form in our times. Yet the darkness of his mythical re-writing of the Bible is matched with hope. Apocalypse could become self-creation, that is, creation by the Self.

Alchemy shows the way, with its myth of helping the god trapped in matter. If we become alchemists, we might help the trapped god—a very dark energy indeed, if it is capable of material incarnation in weapons of mass destruction. By our own individuation, we lead the dark energy of the collective unconscious/God towards a new evocation of the Self, healing some of the dark energy of the godhead. Individuation alchemically refines the black substance of being, now sealed off in our modern weapons.

Symbols turn destructive energy into creative energy. It is just possible that modernity's apocalyptic myth could become *a new creation myth* that would bring back what modernity has denied: the sacred, the body, connection to nature and to love. The imperative for individual and cultural individuation re-aligns the Sky Father and Earth Mother creation myths through the creative use of new and old symbols.

Answer to Job is Jung's demonstration of how creative writing aims for healing, molding the foundational myths of consciousness into a marriage of Sky Father and Earth Mother. He aims to shift the myths from apocalypse to redemption, in which self-creation by the individual (individuation) is creation by the Self. That is, redemption occurs through individuation, as a sick ego experiences itself being reborn through the archetypes of the unconscious. The Self thus creates the new self, in the sense of a new ego identity.

Jung's writing is a form of creativity that weaves its thread of symbols between two mythical visions: of *created* reality and of *creating* reality. The science of symbols unites the creativity of the psyche with history, culture, nature, and cosmos.

FURTHER READING

Paul Bishop, *Jung's Answer to Job: A Commentary* (London and New York: Brunner-Routledge, 2002).

Everything you ever wanted to know about Jung's favorite work; Bishop reveals all.

Roderick Main, ed., *Jung on Synchronicity and the Paranormal* (Princeton, NJ: Princeton University Press, 1997).

Key passages of Jung edited and introduced by a major scholar of Jung's ideas on religion and science.

Roderick Main, *The Rupture of Time: Synchronicity and Jung's Critique of Modern Western Culture* (New York: Brunner-Routledge, 2004).

Main's book on synchronicity and Jung's attitude to religion, science, and modernity is the most complete and persuasive on the subject.

David L. Miller, *Three Faces of God: Traces of the Trinity in Literature and Life* (New Orleans: Spring Journal Books, 2005).

The book is distinguished by Miller's wit and wisdom in relating theology to Jung's notions of the creative psyche. Highly recommended.

Sonu Shamdasani, *Jung and the Making of Modern Psychology: The Dream of a Science* (Cambridge and New York: Cambridge University Press, 2003).

The most thorough examination of Jung in the context of the history of science, written by a distinguished historian.

Ann Belford Ulanov, *The Feminine in Jungian Psychology and Christian Theology* (Evanston, Illinois: Northwestern University Press, 1971).

An early work by an author who has written extensively on religion, gender, and Jungian psychology.

Jung and Power:
Politics and Gender

The Personal is Political

This chapter will look at Jung in a personal light, including his ventures into medical politics in Nazi Germany and his controversial remarks on gender. Yet while considering these flaws in Jung, the man and psychologist, the chapter will also argue that his work offers something significant to modern thinking about both of these painful topics. Eminent post-Jungians, such as Andrew Samuels, have analyzed Jung's political failings as part of the process of generating a new political theory.[1] And while Jung's gender conflicts tax the patience of many contemporary readers, I nonetheless hope to show that his work in this area might yet make a vital contribution to feminism and gender studies.[2]

Jung, the (International) Leader

In the late 1920s, the developing field of psychoanalysis needed an international forum. Germany was the logical base, as most of the original psychoanalysts were from that background, and in 1928, the International General Medical Society for Psychotherapy was founded. Jung was elected its president in 1933—while the Nazis were coming to power.

This was the beginning of an ignominious period for Jung. It is worth remembering the painful fact that Jung's involvement with the Nazis, who seized operating control of the International Society in 1936, was not uninfluenced by his quarrel with Sigmund Freud. Not only was Freud Jewish, but so were many psychoanalysts of his generation—enough for the Nazis to reject psychoanalysis wholesale and condemn Freud's work to be burned. In providing an alternative to Freudian psychoanalysis, Jung was in the morally dangerous position of being considered for favor. His publications were scrutinized for compatibility with Nazi ideas, and he was liable to be cast as "rescuing" depth psychology from its perversion as a "Jewish science."

As president of the International Society, Jung automatically became editor of the Society's journal, the *Zentralblatt fur Psychotherapie*, though actual control was soon seized by the president of the dominant German section of the Society, Professor Matthias Göring, a cousin of the Reichsmarschall. Göring inserted pro-Nazi material in the *Zentralblatt* that Jung later claimed to have known nothing about. Whether or not this was the case, as official editor, he still bore responsibility, as Andrew Samuels argues in *The Political Psyche*.[3]

A further item in the case against Jung also does not indict him directly. The Analytical Psychology Club in Zurich was formed as a social center for patients and analysts. In 1944, a secret clause was added to its bylaws, creating a quota for Jewish membership. Jews could now only make up ten per cent of full members, and twenty-five per cent of guest members. This clause, repealed in 1950, was not instituted by Jung, but nevertheless could not have been enacted contrary to his wishes.[4]

Jung had grown used to the petty struggles and grievances of psychoanalytic politics in earlier years, but his underestimation of the political and social realities of the 1930s is nonetheless culpable. Was it a cultivated naivety that enabled him to retain the presidency of the International Society when, by 1934, it was obvious that the Nazis were not going to leave the Society alone?

Jung did not finally resign his presidency until after the outbreak of war in 1940, and from that moment, his work, too, was banned. At last, an unsavory association was over.

Jung and the Nazis: What Jung Did

It is notable that Jung's position as the Aryan potential savior of psychoanalysis in an anti-Semitic age was first identified by none other than Freud.[5] When the two were still friends, Freud had told Jewish comrades that Jung's support was invaluable in preventing their ideas from being rejected as relevant merely to the psychology of Jews. In the 1930s, Jung gets into a lot of trouble with remarks about "psychological difference" between races, including a supposed Jewish difference. This was, however, a distinction accepted even by Freud.[6]

In 1934, Jung published an article in the *Zentralblatt*, "The State of Psychotherapy Today."[7] Here Jung does indeed make statements about Freud and about the psychology of Jews that could be regarded as anti-Semitic, especially given the ever more terrifying Nazi persecution. He writes, for example, that Freud failed to understand the powerful entity of National Socialism, clumsily adding that the Aryan unconscious has higher potential than the Jewish, and that Jews do not create their own culture but require another as "host" for their activities.[8]

Samuels' analysis draws attention to another unfortunate comparison Jung makes: Jews are physically weaker, like women, and oppose their enemies by looking for cracks in their defences.[9] Another suspect remark comes in a footnote to the 1935 edition of *Two Essays in Psychology*: it would be an error to apply Jewish categories to Germans and Slavs.[10]

Samuels also shows how long-standing is Jung's preoccupation with racial difference. He refers, as far back as a 1918 essay, to the notion that Jews differ significantly from Germanic peoples because they lack the chthonic element of having their own soil under foot.[11] Before the creation of the State of Israel, Jews had no homeland of their own. Culturally, they were identified as wanderers, and Jung believed this deeply affected their psychology.

What Jung also Did

From the distance of the twenty-first century, it is easy to condemn Jung for allowing his bitterness against Freud, his eagerness for international leadership, and his preoccupation with racial differences to allow himself to become associated in any way with anti-Semitism, and to be drawn into even a tacit support of the Nazis. And after the war, Jung never made a straightforward apology for his behavior. But many who accuse Jung of Nazi complicity today regard his record as so tainted as to justify glossing over the more complex realities of the situation, as well as ignoring all Jung's works and ideas.

Jung was head of an international society and allowed Nazi contamination of it. He wrote remarks that could be construed as anti-Semitic, and which, given the context, were inevitably seized upon by the formulators of Nazi propaganda. Crucially, however, he did not go on record as supporting any Nazi *policies*, and he certainly did not endorse the persecution of the Jews. Nothing compelled him, in 1934, to create the protective barrier of an individual membership category for Jewish psychoanalysts in the International Society. Before a critical meeting that year, Jung visited a Jewish lawyer, Vladimir Rosenbaum, a friend and the husband of one of his patients. [12] Jung brought the lawyer evidence that the Nazis were going to have Jewish members excluded from the Society, and Jung wanted its constitution rewritten to protect the Jewish psychoanalysts. Rosenbaum was astonished that a man he revered could really believe that he was capable of outwitting the Nazis. He punned on Jung's name, calling him very *young*, and accused him of a fantasy of wielding effective power. [13] Jung denied that he was deluded. He insisted on trying to trick the Germans.

Eventually Rosenbaum complied, and the thing was done. In Jung's name was inserted a clause stating that members did not have to join a national group as a precondition for joining the International Society, but could join as individual members. Thus, when the German national group expelled its own Jewish members, those psychotherapists could remain members of the International Society and thereby retain their right to practice. And there is more.

Recent research, revealed in Deirdre Bair's excellent book, *Jung: A Biography*, shows that from 1934 on, Jung helped many Jewish refugees enter Switzerland by promising to assume their financial responsibility should they prove destitute. [14] Some people who benefited knew Jung; many did not. Jung also treated many Jewish patients for free once they arrived as refugees.

Astonishingly, it now even appears that Jung became a kind of American spy and psychological advisor during the Second World War, beginning in 1943. Zurich was then full of agents and refugees from all sides. A high-ranking American, Allen W. Dulles, set up a Swiss Listening Post,[15] and Jung became an advisor on the psychology of the German leaders, including Hitler. The Americans knew him as Agent 488.[16]

The historical evidence of the relationship between Jung and the Nazis has proven mixed. So what, if anything, is gained by analyzing the tale?

From Jung to Political Forms: Andrew Samuels

There is not enough space to cover the wide range of Andrew Samuels' contributions to Jungian studies here, including having coined the term "post-Jungian" to indicate not only those writers who come chronologically after Jung, but also those able to criticize and revise him. Rather, I will explore how the insights Samuels derives from analyzing Jung's political record enable fascinating treatments of the subject of politics itself.

Samuels' points out two factors that help explain Jung's apparent weakness in fighting off Nazi influence. First of all, there is the quarrel with Freud, in which personal animus and conceptual dispute can hardly be disentangled. Notably, this entwining of the personal and conceptual is what is elsewhere valuable in Jung, while here it leads him to some questionable decisions. Ultimately, Jung came to grasp what late-twentieth century cultural theory routinely insisted upon, that the observer affects what is observed. Cultural discourses and personal psychologies shape what can be thought and theorized.

This brings us to the second factor, Jung's notion of *theory as subjective confession*, meaning that cultural and national differences are real factors in both the psychology of the living person and psychology as written theory. Jung believed all theory to have a personal dimension; it is inevitably affected by an individual's psychology. So Freud's *personality* is part of psychoanalysis, just as Jung's individuality colors his analytical psychology.

To Samuels, the problem in Jung's thinking on these issues is his confusion of categories: where Jung talks about "racial" difference, he actually means "national" difference, in the sense of each country's unique geographic character.[17] Samuels reveals that notions of geography and landscape contribute significantly to Jung's ideas about psychological makeup. Thus Jewish psychology is different from others' in part because the Jews do not have their own land, while Americans, whatever their national origin or race, all acquire the characteristics of Native Americans because of the influence of the land and the climate, and the proximity of Native Americans themselves.[18]

Both Jung's tenacious assertion of the *subjective* in theory and practice, and his belief in national *psychological differences*, are coherent with later critical theory, such as post-colonialism. Less positively, we have seen that, in the context of psychoanalytic politics in the 1930s, Jung allowed this defensible and indeed progressive attitude toward knowledge to be used in the service of prejudice and worse. Samuels argues, however, that Jung's fascination with the psychology of nationhood and power should not be lost, and his own work has done much to make it possible for post-Jungians to think again in this area.

Political Forms

If one adopts the view, contrary to Marx, that materialism cannot provide a total explanation of society, then where do political ideas come from? How are they passed on? There seems to be an unconscious element in their creation and distribution; they seem to "arrive" or to "arise" in the complexity of individual and institutional interactions.

Samuels himself has devised a theory of *political forms*,[19] and he suggests that a sort of "vitalism" might describe how political forms emerge.[20] Vitalism holds that living things have an inner organizing principle, and this brings it close indeed to Jung's understanding of the psyche as teleological. The social vitalism that Samuels invokes is a sense of group and/or institutional psychology infused with purposefulness, with creativity. This "group mind" would extend to all individuals, yet could not be completely dominated by any single person.

What kind of dynamic principle could be the engine of such a political vitalism? Samuels suggests kinship libido, the bond between family members, linked, in Freud and Jung, to the repression of incest fantasy. It is possible to argue that political energy results from the transformation of incestuous energies from the individual's early years. Samuels points out Jung's gesture in this direction, when he too says that kinship libido keeps "creeds, parties, nations, or states together."[21] (It is important to recall here that Jung's crucial point of departure from Freud was his assertion that libido is essentially mutable, and not necessarily sexual.)

In a previous book, *Jung as a Writer*, I showed how this type of political and psychological theory could also be turned toward literary criticism.[22] What if literature were one method of transmitting political forms, that kinship libido is woven into the mutating political forms of the collective psyche? Shakespeare's *Hamlet* seems to speak to this very point.

What (Really) Happens in *Hamlet*

I am going look at political forms in Shakespeare's *Hamlet*[23], particularly as revealed in the last scene. For a play in which a prince hesitates over the killing of a father-figure, in part due to confused feelings about his mother, an Oedipal explanation would appear inevitable. However, Jungian literary theory and Samuels' notion of political forms together offer another way of exploring the political psyche of the play.

In *Hamlet*, kinship libido might more properly be called "kingship" libido. Hamlet's agony over his father's death is inseparable from his feelings about his father as king. But it is not just personal ambition on the part of young Hamlet; the killing of a king is a particular sacrilege in the political world of the Tudor monarchy, placing a terrible burden on the "true" successor. The personal anguish of Hamlet as beloved son is also the political form-cum-national psychology of sacred kingship. What is, on one level, the intimate experience of every son who outlives his father, on another carries a specific notion of political legitimacy. As presented in the play, a son's grief simultaneously expresses the monarchy as divinely sanctioned patriarchy. *Hamlet* demonstrates the evolution of a political form, from sacred king into politician.

The play is set in a time during which the tradition of the divine right of kings is falling into decay. Decaying rule is suggested first by the arrival of *an-Other* Hamlet—his father, the old king—as a ghost, thus dramatizing the archaic form of Prince Hamlet's self-image. The ghost demands immediate and bloody revenge for his murder, taking no account of such modern conceptions as rule of law or proof of guilt.

A decisive point in the play is reached when the murderer, the now-king Claudius, confesses his guilt before all, but suddenly realizes that

God will not absolve him. For at the root of Claudius' murderous behavior is the power of an ancient fertility myth from before the times of patriarchal kingship, when it was the queen who held power. She would take a new king every year, providing the new contender killed the old king and thereby proved his virility. Such a sexual rite, sealed by blood sacrifice, was thought to ensure the fertility of land and people. Claudius and Gertrude have unconsciously re-enacted this rite.

Shakespeare's *Hamlet*, however, insists that politics must move on from such sacred myth. Gertrude and the other woman in Hamlet's life, Ophelia, who loves him, are both ultimately punished for adopting the goddess role. Her son attacks Gertrude, and Ophelia is swallowed up by the archetypal Earth Mother in a painful madness. What in ancient myth is an evocation of female divinity, is for poor Ophelia her drowning in the darkness of a sacred archetype. She arrives on stage singing crazy songs and madly distributing flowers. Plunging further into the unconscious after she exits, she finally dies by drowning.

Women are pushed back into the mythical unconscious in *Hamlet*. Meanwhile, the young prince must struggle out of it to achieve his transformation from ritual sacrifice to politician. As Shakespeare's audience knew, the traditional response to Old King Hamlet's revelations of murder would have been for the prince to kill Claudius at once, then seize the throne and marry Ophelia. So why doesn't he? The answer suggests that the evolution of political forms requires the mutation of sacred avenger into politician. Immediate revenge is the way of *unconscious* submission to myths that are now outmoded.

What is required is the development of political consciousness, both among the characters on stage and in the play's audience. Hamlet organizes a troupe of travelling players to perform a deliberately allusive play about a murder, thereby revealing Claudius' crimes to the royal court, and revealing to the theater audience the theatrical nature of politics itself. Crucially, Prince Hamlet's growth in consciousness is not the main issue here; it is, rather, that of the *audience*, which participates in—and experiences the transformation of—political consciousness.

When Claudius kneels in prayer and feels no presence of God, he fails to admit *the presence of the audience*. In that scene, the audience is in the position of the divine, of granting or withholding absolution. For the politician (as opposed to the sacred warrior prince who is no longer viable), it will always be the *audience* or the public who will be the true partner in their political career.

The play tells us that the sacred warrior prince is no longer viable because Hamlet's contemporary and rival, Laertes, tries to play that role. Claiming to avenge father and sister, Laertes is drawn into an ignoble plan to kill Hamlet. He represents the failure Hamlet would have been, had he refused the painful growth of consciousness and followed instead the old pattern into the new age.

The play does not demonstrate political forms so much as enact them; the play is *the transformation of political consciousness for a new era.* Consider its final moments: a male dynasty has spectacularly imploded as Fortinbras leads his army to take the throne, while Horatio cradles the dying Prince Hamlet in his arms. Left on stage are two visions of the future, shortly to be manifested in the English Civil War: power through military force, represented by Fortinbras with his army; and the politics of brotherly love, imaged in Hamlet's death in Horatio's embrace.

Moreover, Shakespearean audiences would have recognized the tableau of Hamlet and Horatio in the final scene as a male version of the iconic Christian Virgin Mary cradling her dying Son, an image with still more ancient roots as the earth goddess clasping her dying son-lover. *Hamlet* is ominous for masculine-feminine relations (the only loving embrace between man and woman is when Hamlet leaps into Ophelia's grave), for it is relations between men, and between men and power, that will undergo the next revolution in consciousness. Here, the play teleologically anticipates the revolutionary political forms of the seventeenth century.

Prince Hamlet's true erotic connection to the unconscious has always been through death. At the start of the play, this was archaic in form, when he accepted allegiance to his father's ghost. Then, in his handling of Yorick's skull and by grasping dead Ophelia in his arms, he rehearses his own transformation from play-acting clown and lover to something that can not be fully expressed in his age. Freud might recognize an example of the death drive and stop there, but Jungian theory and Samuels' notion of political forms see something more complex, more culturally embedded and more numinous in this turn to death as the "undiscovered country," signifying the unknown future.

Indeed, death at the end of the play is *symbolic* in the Jungian sense. As a symbol, death marks the change from a religiously-sanctioned form of government to a secular one, from sacred warrior to politician. Death as a symbol also permits the play's transformation of the consciousness of its audience. Jungian theory considers art to be a form of active intervention in a culture's psychological evolution, a collective transformation of consciousness, including that of politics and power.

Gender and a Man with Two Wives

To turn from politics to gender is to enter another controversial dimension of Jung's life and work. A glimpse of Jung's unorthodox romantic life provides some useful context. As a young married doctor, Jung had affairs, including a significant relationship with a former patient, Sabina Spielrein, who later became a Freudian psychoanalyst.[24]

Jung's long relationship with another former patient, Toni Wolff, resulted in an unusual public arrangement. Bair records that Jung told his wife, Emma, that he must treat Toni as his "other wife."[25] Toni came regularly to meals, and the children were instructed to call her "aunt."[26] Jung would spend weekends alone with Toni at Bollingen Tower, his spiritual and creative retreat near Zurich, or they would travel abroad for meetings. At home in Zurich, Jung would often arrive at events with both Emma and Toni.

The five Jung children grew up bitterly resenting Toni Wolff and the hurt she caused their mother. Not surprisingly, Emma seriously considered a divorce,[27] but for whatever private reasons, chose not to end the marriage. Both Emma Jung and Toni Wolff became respected Jungian analysts. Jung remained in a relationship with Toni from 1914 until her death in 1953, and Emma died in 1955. Jung carved a memorial to both women on a stone at Bollingen.

A Conservative (on Women) with Revolutionary Ideas (on Gender)

On gender and the feminine, Jung has the problem of being a conservative with some nonetheless revolutionary ideas. From the perspective of his "subjective confession," he is reluctant to support women attempting to change patriarchy. On a personal level, he is content with the traditional—many would say, outmoded—social structures that relegated woman to the roles of wife and mother, despite his professional support of women as analysts. On the matter of the feminine, however, especially if defined as a component of the male psyche, it was quite a different matter. For the feminine was a topic of supreme importance that fired his imagination all his life.

To begin, we need to establish the *essentialism* of Jung's position on gender before moving to the paradox of his profound *anti-essentialism*. It will then be possible to clarify what is problematic about Jung's ideas on gender, and what is gloriously productive.

The essentialist Jung saw no problem with traditional gender arrangements, because gender was a simple matter of characteristics pertaining to male or female bodies. Masculinity resided in men and femininity in women. Both genders remained suitable for their separate roles. This unthinking Jung was happy to make pronouncements about men and women that assumed an unchanging essential gender identity proper to each. For example, *this* Jung said that eros and logos were merely helpful concepts, while simultaneously attributing logos to a man's superior powers of rationality and eros to a woman's ability to connect through feeling. In revealing language, eros is the "true nature" of women while their logos is a "regrettable accident."[28] None of this attribution is supplied with any substance apart from an essentialist assumption of what Woman is!

Here as elsewhere, however, Jung's fundamental attitude to knowledge, his epistemological stance, will not let the topic rest so placidly. What is of overriding importance to Jung is the founding creativity and mystery of the archetypal unconscious. One of the chief ways that the unconscious affects our lives, he believed, is through gender. So the unconscious will actively challenge the ego by assuming styles of gender foreign to it.

Drawing these styles of feminine and masculine from the ego's experience in historical time, the unconscious will display archetypal images of the "opposite" gender. Women will discover a mysterious masculinity becoming manifest within, attributed by this Jung to a figure of archetypal activity he called the "animus." Men detect an inner femininity, which he termed the result of an "anima."

Two consequences emerge from this portrayal of innate gender fluidity. Firstly, Jung's essentialism must fall away before this more significant assertion of the creative unconscious, for it will constantly disrupt and re-make the ego's gender through individuation. Secondly, however the conservative Jung might quail, such a psychic processing of gender represents a deep subversion of patriarchal gender arrangements.

Since everything rests upon the creative unconscious, the challenge to the ego's gender bias is ultimately a challenge to cultural gender bias. In a world in which the feminine has been historically devalued, the unconscious task of fertilizing the ego in individuation takes on the historical task of evicting patriarchy. A healthy ego (in both sexes) requires strengthening individual women and their cultural valuation.

Thus we see Jung pulled two ways in his writing. On both an individual and social level, he is torn between his personal preference for traditional social arrangements and the revolutionary direction of his theory. Indeed, what he came to regard as his most significant insights into the feminine prefigured nothing less than *a re-making of the symbols of religion* in modernity!

Later in his career, Jung became fascinated by gender as a historical psychological phenomenon. Modernity, he believed, was sick because, with the triumph of rationality, it had excluded so much that seemed Other. The modern secular West was the direct inheritor of a Christian culture that had progressively devalued feminine symbolism. Jung recognized, with other critics of patriarchy, that the "feminine" had been used symbolically as a means of rejecting uncomfortable matters by deeming them inherently undesirable. It had been made to stand for sexuality, body, connectedness, the unconscious, irrationality, and matter itself.

So fierce did this suppression become that the result gave rise to a formidable shadow. Jung argued that our world was in deep peril from "an-Other," powerful precisely *because of* centuries of patriarchal rejection. He saw in weapons of mass destruction the revenge of despised "feminine" matter. Using such weapons is, in mythical terms, the vengeance of the dark divine that had been repressed for too long (see Chapter 5).

Put another way, Jung was well aware that the modern world was the offspring of an unbalanced relationship between the two gendered creation myths (see Chapter 3). Sky Father had triumphed all too thoroughly, and his paradigm based on separation, dualism, and rationality conceived as bodiless spirit had eclipsed Earth Mother's body, sexuality, animism, and consciousness-through-connectedness.

At almost every level, Jung's psychology is an attempt to re-balance these myths. Individuation is about a *process* in which consciousness is made through both separation from *and* connection to the Other. Synchronicity attempts to join principles of knowledge from Earth Mother with Sky Father's rational science. Jung's Self is on the one hand associated with Christian symbolism of Christ and God, while on the other hand, the Self must unite the inner Others—body and spirit, anima and animus—in a "syzygy" that incorporates sexuality into the sacred.

Jung is a gender revolutionary in terms of cultural symbolism. At least four volumes of his *Collected Works* are devoted to the history of symbolism that carries a psychological charge. His exhaustive analysis of alchemy texts was devoted to recovering symbols that he believed embodied what mainstream Christianity had discarded. He wrote about alchemy's respect for the body and about the natural sacredness alchemy accorded to animals, and he delighted in alchemy's celebration of sexual congress, its goal of symbolic "conjunction." This represented a wealth of vibrant psychic matter that official religion had rejected by determining the feminine to be inferior.

So Jung can be enlisted as a gender radical at a collective level. His personal difficulties, on the other hand, do provide something "Other" than irritation in his writing.

The Feminine and Jung's Writing

The anima has an erotic, emotional character, the animus a rationalising one. Hence most of what men say about feminine eroticism, and particularly about the emotional life of women, is derived from their own anima projections and distorted accordingly. On the other hand, the astonishing assumptions and fantasies that women make about men come from the activity of the animus, who produces an inexhaustible supply of illogical arguments and false explanations.[29]

These are three extraordinarily interesting sentences. Each comes from a different perspective, yet their interrelationship is fascinating. The first sentence, describing the primary characteristics of anima and animus, is conceptual and rational; its author could be of either gender. The second sentence is written from the position of men looking at women, and tells us that a man's view of women is distorted by his inner feminine, his anima.

Then the third sentence bursts upon the reader. It seems so uncontrolled! The need to convict women as more unreasonable than men is so overwhelming. "Who" is speaking in the third sentence? *From the logic of the writing itself, the speaker must be Jung's anima!* In these three sentences we have a slippage. First comes lofty conceptuality "above" a single gender position. Then the embodied voice of a man who concedes the influence upon him of an irrational anima. Finally comes an outcry about women so driven by irrational energy that it betrays itself *as* the anima. For does not the third sentence overtly illustrate the point of the second, that men cannot be objective about women? Is it not, truly, a loss of control on the part of the rational scientist? Such a moment is a wonderful illustration of the many voices within Jung's writing. Moreover, it demonstrates how the unconscious, here labeled the feminine, challenges fixed meanings. This is not the mere undoing of meaning, however; rather, the unconscious feminine is *productive of meaning*, showing meaning to be a process, and one that is ongoing. This sort of writing *enacts* the feminine as both the source of, and constant challenge to, theory.

Anima in the Theory

... I once asked myself, "What am I really doing?"... Whereupon a voice within me said, "It is art."... I knew for a certainty that the voice had come from a woman ...[30]

After the traumatic quarrel with Freud, and enduring great mental distress, Jung experienced vivid dreams and visions that he was later to identify as the true source of some of his theories, including that of the anima. One of these encounters was with a feminine voice, which notably refuses to cooperate with Jung's inner commands. Jung portrays her as a nagging woman, yet "she" is the source of his most imaginative insights!

There is more to this persistent feminine voice, for her arrival mimics the circumstances of the woman who provided key material for his doctoral thesis, his teenage cousin, Helene Preiswerk, who claimed to be able to communicate with the dead. In Jung's thesis, he writes about Preiswerk, whom he calls "Miss S.W.," manifesting a number of spirits, including a very impressive woman called Ivenes.[31] Later, Jung himself takes the position of medium in allowing "the anima" to take over his own written voice.

F. X. Charet was the first to write about the importance of Jung's thesis to his later intellectual development in *Spiritualism and the Foundations of C. G. Jung's Psychology* (1993).[32] Charet points out that ideas such as the anima and the Self are present in embryo in the thesis, even though it was written well before Jung had formulated his own psychology.

What Charet does not consider is the gender politics of Jung taking up the feminized position of the medium. In the highly gendered structure of the doctoral thesis, we have an authoritative male scientist analyzing a passive female subject. The feminine speaks, but only as medium, not in her own voice but *for* some Other. Later, when Jung assumes the medium position himself, the voice of the feminine is again marginalized. He relates to the feminine anima not as to an autonomous being but rather as to an "inner Other," a mere *aspect* of "his" psyche.

The doctoral thesis does, however, offer something more to the figure of feminine-as-Other than a progressive marginalization. With Jung, it is always the case that his foundational principle of the creative unconscious sometimes results in surprises, or even reversals. For the doctoral thesis contains two anima figures: one is Ivenes, but the other is the young medium herself, Preiswerk/Miss S. W., who has been diagnosed as mentally ill as in order to "explain" her extraordinary imaginative productions.

Jung decides to invoke an authority he had not yet met at the time, Sigmund Freud, and interpret her "spirits" as due to "nothing but" her adolescent sexuality.[33] Here is Jung the proto-Freudian, anticipating his future relation with the great psychoanalyst. Yet here, also, is the future dissenter from Freud's insistence on sexuality as the sole root of psychic imagination, for Jung is unable to suppress his excitement at the specific imaginative *content* of S.W.'s visions.

Investigator Jung is especially fascinated by S.W.'s most impressive "spirit," a mature woman called Ivenes, whose enigmatic personality is at the heart of the astonishing stories. In séances, S.W. as Ivenes tells long tales of erotic adventures, including past lives in which Ivenes had been romantically entwined with Jung himself. Ivenes and S.W. also espouse "Mystic Science," an apparent attempt to unite the Book of Genesis and Darwin, in which the human race is said to be descended from *both* monkeys and Adam. Additionally, Ivenes' fertile narratives invoke the literary genres of ghost story, gothic, and romance, as well as a science fiction fable that re-imagines how the Earth might relate to the other planets.[34]

In this thesis, the young researcher forces himself into what he clearly considers to be the "correct" attitude of scientific rationality, while unconscious creativity emerges through the figures of the real woman and her imaginal visitor. I would argue that this is not just a matter of recognizing both S.W. and Ivenes as anima images for Jung himself, but rather that they embody *the anima images of Jung's future work*, the figures that lure him toward his future exploration of psychic depths, passions, and visions of the cosmos.

As well as being at once childish and richly creative, the figure of S.W./ Ivenes as anima *is the unconscious of theory, its irrational eros*. The feminine figure as at once the young medium and the fascinating reincarnated "spirit" is the creative, "image-inative" energy behind or below Jung's (masculine) rational psychology. Where a male person has an anima, I am arguing that a logos-dominated theory has its Other in the eros-driven, embodied, sexual, unconscious psyche. In fact, if we imagine psychology-as-theory as if it were an ego entity, we can see S.W. summoning Ivenes as a figure of anima as *consciousness-as-related-to-unconsciousness*. The writing of S.W. in Jung's thesis is *psychology-as-related-to-unconsciousness*.

To summarize: Jung's doctoral thesis contains two types of writing. One mode—defined by the medical and historical context, and by Jung's later analysis of modernity (as unbalanced due to the dominance of ego-consciousness)—is masculine and determined to stay in the realm of the rational. The other mode might be called *anima writing*. S.W.'s pronouncements and visions, and the other voices she calls spirits, including Ivenes, tell stories of what the modern world lacks. She *imagines* or *images* a way of reconciling the recent material sciences, such as Darwinism, with psychic necessities such as eros, body, sexuality, romance, story, and fiction. These "feminine" forms offer multiple threads for connecting to the cosmos.

Arguably, Jung spends his entire career attempting to unravel S.W.'s visions and to unite these two types of writing. I believe that S.W. represented his initial attempt to weave the voice of the creative Other into his writing, an-Other that, for him, was forever feminine—that which can never entirely be understood or controlled. Jung takes over S.W.'s superb evocation of the feminine as creativity. For S.W. as anima, as the unconscious of Jungian theory, *is* its connective, erotic, unpredictable, living reality in the psyche. What she represents conceptually in his thesis becomes a living source for the development of Jung's own psychology-as-related-to-unconsciousness. Here the writing itself is a healing medicine.

Jung depicts a feminine of supreme importance to the future of mankind. Yet still he persists in tying her to the masculine by conceptualizing her as anima, and therefore necessarily relating to a masculine ego. Of course, the presence of the Earth Mother is *felt* in S.W.'s magnificent stories of erotic intrigue, in which sacred and scientific writing are *connected*. The anima is Jung's attempt to domesticate the nature goddess in his writing, to confine her into a concept, to seal her into this device of separation and logos. However, as we have seen, Earth Mother powers of eros and connectivity refuse to be *rationalized*. Jung the conservative is menaced by a psychic creativity that he can neither control, nor pretend that it is therapeutic to control. Jung the healer attempts to weave this ancient goddess into modernity in his psychology writing.

We need to take Jung's gender thinking further. For if there is a Jung who thought women naturally belonged in the home, there is also a Jung whose profound criticism of patriarchy as a distortion of the human soul could make a vital contribution to feminist theory.

Jung for Feminism?
Replacing the Patriarchal Symbolic

Feminist theory tries to understand the deep structures that have demeaned and marginalized women. One of the most influential sources for such research has been Freudian and Lacanian psychoanalysis. Problematically, however, Freud privileged the penis as the organ defining the superiority of the male. Lacan revised Freud's emphasis on the literal body, resulting in more sophisticated, gendered notions of language and culture. For Lacan, the crucial Oedipal split that creates ego and unconscious is the child's entry into language.

Thus the phallus, as sign of masculinity, is the emblem of privilege. Male and female children take up a different relation to the phallus, yet neither gender "has" it. This is because the phallus represents the fullness of power and completion, which no person can possess once the split from the maternal unconscious has occurred. So the masculine "has" the phallus only ambivalently, while the feminine must "be" the phallus for the masculine.

The Lacanian Symbolic Order is the combined language and codes of a particular culture; it organizes our consciousness into the various forms of social discourse. It is *patriarchal* because the phallus is the privileged signifier, to which every human being, both male and female, must relate if they are to function within the culture. Jung, however, undoes that masculine privilege.

We recall that the Jungian unconscious actively brings forth the child's ego. Whereas the Freudian treatment of the Oedipus complex emphasizes the repression of forbidden sexuality to structure the ego-unconscious relation, Jung stresses that the psyche is innately creative, autonomous, and active. Hence the separation of the ego in the formation of the child is, for Jung, more an active partnership than for Freud. Separation is negotiated between, firstly, a mother archetype in the unconscious pushing away the ego and, secondly, a drive within the ego to form a distinct and boundaried psychic being. For the latter, Jung conceded the relevance of an Oedipus complex derived from relating to parents. For the reason of the different understanding of ego separation between Jung and Freud/Lacan, the Jungian notion of the "symbolic" differs from the

Lacanian Symbolic Order. The Jungian is primarily rooted in the efforts of the unconscious to create meaning through becoming embodied in an ego in the world. The meaning-making principles that dwell in the unconscious Jung called archetypes, for example, anima and animus, which are "archetypal" in their numinous power and boundless creativity. Most importantly for our purposes here, the Jungian unconscious is as capable of generating strong, even divine feminine images and meaning as it is of producing masculine symbols.

The unconscious inevitably tries to counteract individual or cultural bias in its efforts to forge a relationship between its creative impulses and the socialized ego. A society may therefore inherit patriarchal structures, but because the individual unconscious is endowed with archetypal androgyny, it will naturally find itself combating patriarchal dominance. Individuation, which has now come to encompass gender fluidity, thus inherently challenges patriarchy.

The "Jungian symbolic" cannot be patriarchal or biased toward the masculine, whatever Jung the historically-bound individual might have preferred. For Jung's notion of psyche inherently resists gender distortions. In terms of the religious symbolism that Jung believed should regulate the psyche, divine images must be feminine *as well as* masculine.

James Hillman: Releasing the Anima

One of the most influential developers of Jung's legacy is James Hillman, whose many books and important innovations cannot be summarized here (see Further Reading). In the 1970s, Hillman proposed a radical transformation of Jung's anima.[35] Through a critical re-examination of Jung's texts, Hillman succeeded in detaching the anima from Jung's delight in opposites. No longer limited to men, "she" should adopt Jung's other name for her (indeed her name in English translation), "soul," and take her true position as a structure of consciousness-in-relationship-to-unconsciousness *in both sexes*. Now the anima could fully inhabit her role as relatedness, as the bridge to the unknown psyche, and not be automatically associated with real people in their literal genders.

Hillman then proposed that Eros, a male figure in Greek mythology, be differentiated from anima and recognized as a separate principle of sexuality. Eros should not be falsely linked to the anima in her femininity, as Jung had proposed. Thus women need no longer carry the anima or soul for men, having their own anima-souls to cherish. Similarly, both men and women have equal access to animus or spirit.

Taking this revised notion of anima a stage further, Hillman argues that anima as relatedness to the unconscious is *the true basis of consciousness*. This serves to de-center the ego as foundation of consciousness. Hillman traces the elevation of the ego back to the culture of the masculine hero myth. "He," the ego, is driven by the desire to conquer and subdue the Other. And while this approach is psychologically useful in childhood and adolescence, the hero myth needs to be left behind by the adult who discovers his/her true existence in anima-relatedness.

Hillman situates the anima as the archetype of psychology and soul-making, who can appear as one or as many. Anima and animus are the psychic lenses by which the Other is known, so if the anima is sometimes understood as "one," that is not to be taken as her essence. Rather we should realize that she is being regarded through a perspective conditioned to see "ones." In healthy soul-making, it is the proper role of anima and animus to unite in an inner marriage.

Hillman's revisions of gender and the anima are exciting, opening up possibilities that build upon those first explored by Jung. For Jung's thinking on gender is the point where reason and theory are defeated, as his mingled essentialism and radical opening up of gender notions combine to demonstrate.

Where Hillman transforms Jung's primary image of the feminine, the anima, Ginette Paris has given remarkable and radical treatment to the gender of his narratives. From writing that explicitly draws upon those brave survivors of the Earth Mother in the goddesses of classical Greece in *Pagan Meditations*,[36] to an enchanting *realization* of the embodied feminine in intellectual history in *Wisdom of the Psyche*,[37] Paris' innovations are psychically rich and form an important contribution to depth psychology. While space considerations preclude greater treatment here, I want to stress how Paris' work augments Hillman's on the anima. Hillman recuperates the feminine as *image* and Paris, the feminine as *narrative*; together, these creative developments of Jung's ideas offer truly groundbreaking ways of rethinking gender, power, and culture.

Jung: Power, Politics, and Gender

This chapter has looked at Jung's encounters with politics, when his career came up against the horrific realities of 1930s Germany, and with the more systemic functions of power through gender. In both cases, politics and gender, the dangers and disadvantages of Jung's attempt to live and write as a whole person, as an embodied subjective being as well as a rational theorist, are apparent. Jung's failings over politics and gender center on his over-confidence in the *situatedness* of his writing, that is, in the way he allows personal impulses to inhabit and inform his writing—sometimes carelessly, sometimes flagrantly provocatively. He points out, rightly, that all theory is at least in part subjective. Unfortunately, he sometimes allows "subjective" to excuse subjecting the reader to his biases! His failings reveal the danger of allowing his own unconscious impulses into his writing, of allowing his own animus and woundedness to influence his theorizing.

Yet Jung allows himself this license because he never abandoned his fundamental attitude to knowledge: that it must take into account the creativity and partial unknowability of the unconscious. Personal and cultural flaws enact the psyche's foundational grappling with the unknown. In terms of career and writing, one might say that Jung took too many risks, and that his personal weaknesses were expressed in outright anti-Semitism and misogyny. Taking another view, I argue that Jung's flaws, while deserving of criticism, do not finally detract from the potential value of his ideas. Indeed, I point out that post-Jungians such as Andrew Samuels and James Hillman have produced important new cultural analyses by exploring the cracks and contradictions in Jung's ideas.

A third response to Jung's positions on politics, gender, and power is also possible. What Jung forces us to acknowledge is that it is precisely in reading "the difficult bits," when anger and passion are aroused, that we are *opened up to our own psyche* and thereby forced to confront our own irrational reactions. I suggest that what is most illuminating is how Jung's writing embodies a tension between its conservative and revolutionary nature. Jung both conceptualizes limitless possibility for social change through connection with the creative unconscious, and simultaneously provides a mirror for the darker, more regressive aspects of the soul.

Throughout this book, I have sought to show that Jung offers his writing as a collaboration with the reader. As well as a Sky Father-modeled reading of his rational abstract concepts, we are offered an Earth Mother reading that privileges connectedness and feeling. I would suggest that the invitation to the reader to co-create meaning is most significant because it implicates our own gender anxieties and attitudes to power. Ultimately, we are called to help right a gendered imbalance between masculine and feminine aspects of modernity. Here is revealed most clearly the importance of Jung's invitation to participate in the embodiment of the creative psyche; for here we have an invitation to be inspired, in-spirited, to re-make the social and political world.

FURTHER READING

Sue Austin, *Women's Aggressive Fantasies: A Post-Jungian Exploration of Self-Hatred, Love and Agency* (London and New York: Routledge, 2005).
Austin brings an analyst's perspective to clinical study and a theorist's perspective to the feminist revision of Jung.

F.X. Charet, *Spiritualism and the Foundations of C.G. Jung's Psychology* (New York: SUNY, 1993).
A fascinating exploration of the role of spiritualism in Jung's ideas.

Christine Downing, *Women's Mysteries: Towards a Poetics of Gender* (New York: Crossroad Books, 1993).
Downing has written extensively and with immense depth about myth and gender.

James Hillman, "Anima I," in *Spring: A Journal of Archetype and Culture* (Dallas, TX: Spring Publications, 1973): 97-132, and "Anima II" in *Spring: A Journal of Archetype and Culture* (Dallas, TX: Spring Publications, 1974): 113-146.
In delightfully engaging prose, Hillman makes the case for revising Jung's anima concept.

Aryeh Maidenbaum and Stephen Martin, eds., *Lingering Shadows: Jungians, Freudians and Anti-Semitism* (Boston: Shambhala, 1991).
An important collection of research into Jung's political and cultural associations with Nazi Germany.

Ginette Paris, *Pagan Meditations: Aphrodite, Hestia, Artemis* (Woodstock, CT: Spring Publications Inc., 1986).
Through expert scholarly study of myth, Paris creates a truly imaginative and liberating feminist perspective for the modern woman.

Ginette Paris, *Wisdom of the Psyche: Depth Psychology after Neuroscience* (London and New York: Routledge, 2007).

This remarkable book is truly a work of wisdom for the twenty-first century. It combines the personal, theoretical, and clinical to explore the challenges facing the modern person.

Andrew Samuels, *The Political Psyche* (London and New York: Routledge, 1993).

Samuels' groundbreaking theoretical and clinical delineating of this important new field. Contains significant research on Jung and Germany.

Andrew Samuels, *Politics on the Couch: Citizenship and the Internal Life* (London: Profile Books, 2001).

A profound and witty exploration of the psyche in politics and the politics of psyche. This book is accessible and thought-provoking.

William Shakespeare, *The Tragicall History of Hamlet Prince of Denmarke*, G. Holderness and B. Loughrey, eds. (New York and London: Harvester Wheatsheaf, 1992).

Jung in the Twenty-First Century: Fishing at the Gates of Hell

A Vision

In 1944, Jung had a vision of the whole Earth bathed in luminous beauty.[1] He said that the globe, brimming with a blue radiance, was the most beautiful thing he had ever seen. High in space, peaceful and happy, he entered an ancient temple carved in rock. There he felt himself losing what felt like inessential parts of his being and becoming indescribably fulfilled. He was being prepared for something mysterious and wonderful.

Then there came a sudden change of mood. He was summoned back to Earth by his doctor in the form of a priest-like figure. Brought close to death, Jung was not, after all, going to die of his heart attack. There was more work to do. Between 1944 and Jung's death in 1961, he wrote his most experimental works on the problem of evil, on science and society, and on psyche, nature, and cosmos. In particular, he pondered why modernity had opened the gates of hell.

The Problem of Now: Science and the Open Gates of Hell

After the Second World War, Jung could cite plenty of evidence for his pessimism about Western modernity. As Chapter 6 showed, he himself was involved in the ugly politics of psychoanalysis before the war. He now, of course, was horrified by what had been revealed about the full reality of Nazi atrocities, such as the death camps. Also, as noted in Chapter 5, Jung saw the development of weapons of mass destruction as mythically expressing the dark shadow of the god of the present age: matter, or rather, materialism.

In *Answer to Job*, he had tried to address the post-Christian psyche's entrapment in the Christian apocalyptic narrative.[2] Once religious symbols fail to keep society healthy through a productive relationship between sacred and profane, the story descends into literalism, as the Biblical Apocalypse foretold in the Book of Revelation becomes all too literal in nuclear holocaust.

The only remedy is to change the myth. So a myth of apocalypse needs to be re-framed as a myth of self-creation—a new creation by the Jungian Self. Jung's call for a new myth, for new symbolism suited to a new creative science of the soul, has been answered by other researchers. In twenty-first century ecological thought, an-Other story emerges, speaking of a science of the whole. This final chapter will look at Jung's work in relation to the new scientific paradigm of holism, which includes ideas of "complexity," "emergence," and a creativity in nature that is continuous with humanity.

Such a perspective links Jung to our time by means of this new culture of the *whole*. I will show how Jung's vision of the creative psyche embedded in nature is being developed after him, for example, through recent notions of imagination and the cosmos, a new alignment to non-human nature, and a developing soul-oriented approach to learning. The twenty-first century also brings forth an-Other alchemy in the form of the World Wide Web, accompanied by a renewed understanding of the mythical animation of matter in technology and the development of new digital art.

To explore these ideas, however, we first of all need to recover one of Jung's favorite mythical characters, the Trickster—he of hellish pursuits!

Facing the Culture of the Future

The Trickster and the Anti-Christ

Jung redoubled his study of alchemy in his later years, considering it a symbolic system well suited to understanding the psyche as a whole. Crucially, alchemy as a historical phenomenon took the dark side of the self seriously, while Jung felt that Christianity had become inadequate when it determined that God was only good and that evil was merely the absence of good, with no independent reality of its own.

Jung's God, on the other hand, could be truly dark, even deliberately evil, as in his torture of the hapless Job. This God required the active participation of human beings in order to become more conscious. Only by increasing the consciousness of God—or, to put it another way, through human individuation—could "he" restrain his tendency to inflict his evil upon the world (see Chapter 5). From this perspective, nuclear weapons represent the failure of God/the Self to become conscious, so the dark remains unacknowledged and therefore uncontained.

In alchemy, Jung discovered a figure that he felt best represented the psychic mutability of good and evil. Alchemy calls him Mercurius, the "character" of mercury or quicksilver; other cultures have named him the Trickster or the Fool. Jung noted that alchemy's greater psychic range than orthodox Christianity was matched in pre-Renaissance Europe by a social space being set aside for the Trickster.

The Trickster was the motley star of carnivals, and although some of these survive today, Jung was pessimistic about the continuing psychic potency of the Trickster figure. He believed that the culture of the carnival, with its reversals of hierarchy and celebration of the body, had not endured sufficiently to keep the Trickster psychically alive in modernity. Instead of valuing the Trickster, he says, we have opened the gates of hell.[3]

The Trickster, it seems, serves to keep those gates shut. He helps to preserve the boundary between the dark side of the psyche and the light by being the figure who is able to cross it, thereby enabling consciousness of the dark and preventing the psyche—individual or collective—from being overwhelmed. Thus the Trickster is not a force for good, as we normally understand it. As Mercurius in alchemy, he is even, shockingly, the relation between those Christian polar opposites, Christ and Anti-

Christ, God and Devil. The Trickster crosses all the social and ethical boundaries, *in order that we may perceive them*. His stories show an unreliable figure, not fully human, not quite animal, not quite divine. He is not even securely "he," because the Trickster is unreliable in all things, even gender, as Jung grudgingly admits.

Shortly after the publication of *Answer to Job*, Jung wrote "On the Psychology of the Trickster Figure."[4] Based on a study of the Winnebago cycle of Trickster stories, this small text brings together those elements that psychic symbols require for true potency: the dimensions of space and time.

Jung describes the social function of the Native American Trickster as keeping the collective alert to the darker side of the psyche, yet Jung's real topic is the symbolism of European culture, in which the Trickster lived as the Fool and the Clown of the Carnivals. In alchemy, he was Mercurius, who could incarnate the Virgin Mother or even Satan. This figure even materialized in Church services worshipping donkeys! By means of a figure capable of such transgressions, the medieval psyche came to know its proper bounds.

Jung was profoundly convinced of the historical character of psychological meaning. Symbols and myths could become worn out, yet they still represented a psychic *resonance*. In this sense a conservative, he believed that a re-vitalization of the old myth was needed, not something wholly new. Jung's prescription was too radical for many, however, for it included a renewal of religious symbolism through Mercurius or the Trickster, a rediscovery of feminine in the divine, a muted evocation of the Earth Mother, and an active principle of evil.

To Jung, these so-called "revolutions" actually represented a re-imagining of historical symbols, their iconic importance secured through a reinvigoration of the psyche of the past. (Here it is important to remember that Jungian archetypes are not, despite the historical dimension of the psyche, inherited images or ideas, but rather represent only the potential for similar images to manifest in different cultures and times.)

Moreover, the psyche has dimensions—ultimately unmappable—in space as well as in time. The "Trickster" essay is a good example of this notion because it brings together the "space" of an-Other culture with the historical time of the Trickster in Europe. Of course, Jung does tend to fall into the trap of simply equating a non-Western culture (here, the Winnebago) with the past of Europe, thereby implying a thoroughly colonial attitude toward the "primitive" Other, who is "behind" the level of Western progress. A writer as devoted as Jung to exposing the sickness of his own world, however, would never rest content with such a facile assumption.

In the "Trickster" essay, Jung shows that Winnebago culture and medieval Europe both possessed a psychic sophistication that modernity has lost. Indeed, as the maker of culture and ethics, the Trickster is a supremely *cultured* figure. What modernity is left without, Jung says, is some collective form through which to apply the magic healing of imagination to our own tendency toward evil. The result, Jung writes, is the soldier who does not develop his *own* sense of ethics.[5] The Nazi functionary who says "I was only obeying orders" is the typical soul-less modern person in a culture without the Trickster.[6] No wonder Jung felt that the gates of hell had been left open. But if we, through our rejection of the Trickster, have failed to keep shut the gates of hell, it is now worth taking a look at that infernal region.

Hell is in the North

Medieval Christians were taught to believe in three supernatural regions: Heaven for the Blessed, with Christ, his Virgin Mother, and God; Hell, the abode of Satan, who tortured the souls of evildoers for eternity; and Purgatory, a sort of "halfway-house." In apocryphal scriptures, Christ "harrows hell," descending into the infernal regions briefly to offer hope to the damned. Yet despite Christ's journey to the underworld, the firm demarcation between the regions remains.

Whereas Christian teaching set up a fixed geography of the eternal realms, alchemy did not. Jung believed that alchemy was a symbolic system flexible enough to act as Trickster to Christianity's overly rigid structures, for like the Trickster, alchemy delighted in paradox. Indeed, the alchemists often went so far as to identify hell with the North Pole. In Jung's late work, *Aion*, he explores this northern character of hell.[7]

"Hell in the North" is a geographical expression of the paradoxes of the divine. For if the absolute reality of evil cannot be excluded from God/Self, then neither can God be kept out of hell. A hellfire in the ice is a physical rendering of the denial of the orthodox construction of hell as a region abandoned by God. Here freezing ice writes the pain of abandonment on the vulnerable human body. Lucifer is named for light; he fell from heaven to make his home in the North, and is associated with the frozen region at the height of his powers.[8] In the North, God's love glows in the hellfire.[9]

Alchemical fire, that vital, transforming, perfecting, and destroying power, has a double aspect. In one form, it is the infernal fires of hell.[10] Yet being double, we should not be surprised to learn that the fires of the North Pole contain the heart of Mercurius.[11] We journey by means of the Pole Star; physical travel is but the material dimension of a mystic journey that also turns on the North Pole. From here, the globe appears as a mandala. The North Pole is the true heart of the physical/spiritual journeys of life.

Jung reiterates that the hidden god lives at the North Pole, showing himself in the force of magnetism, guiding travelers who use a compass.[12] Mercurius is synonym for the hidden god, who infuses the whole world from the North Pole. This means that the world is driven by the fires of hell in the North.[13] Hell is a network of psychic or divine powers confounding notions of upper and lower. Jung sees in this vision of hell in the North a mandala pattern of wholeness and order. He says:

> The centering of the image on hell, which is at the same time God, is grounded on the experience that highest and lowest both come from the depths of the soul ...[14]

"Hell in the North" is Jung's invocation of the truly deep abysm in psychic space-time, where the Trickster can be found as the holy figure of Mercurius. Northern hell provides *matter* for the paradoxical Tricksterish imagination, because of its vision of physical and psychic space as one.

Theologian David L. Miller has developed Jung's linking of infernal powers with the imagination in his book, *Hells and Holy Ghosts*.[15] Hell, he argues, is a necessary function of the imagination: it is engine to the soul. We will return to the imaginative potency of hell and the North at the end of this chapter.

Going Back to Where We Started: Myths of Form and Matter

Jung believed that modernity was sick because it had excluded so much that was Other. His writing tries to undo some of that exclusion by its reverence for mystery, by the notion of an ethical working *with* nature rather than *upon* it, and by exploring those attitudes and beliefs arrogantly discarded by modern rationalism. Western structures of inclusion and exclusion, Jung shows, originate in the great founding creation myths.

Western science has a mechanical view of the universe based upon causality and separation. Ultimately, this idea can be traced back to the monotheistic patriarchal interpretation of the Book of Genesis. Becoming the dominant strand in Western Christendom, the myth of the Sky Father privileges separation and transcendence of the body. It does so because it stems from the notion that God created nature as separate from himself. Hence, mind is conceived as separate from matter. Consciousness is based on discrimination and separation from unconscious Other.[16]

As feminist scholars have shown, Genesis is capable of "Other" readings that show the legacy of an Earth Mother religion. Here the earth "herself" is sacred and generates all life, including humanity, in an interdependent web. Body and sexuality are also sacred, and consciousness is based upon connection to the Other. Earth is a mother goddess, but "she" is not merely the feminine. "She" is prior to the splitting into two genders, an animistic whole embodying multiplicity of being. "She" is the potential for plurality in gender and culture figured in a *web of connection* rather than a binary structure of hierarchy and exclusion.

The sickness of Western modernity lies in the way these two great myths of consciousness have lost touch with each other. The repression of the Earth Mother is manifested in the exploitation of nature and the marginalization of the feminine, the devaluing of non-rational psychic forms, and the repression of the unconscious—all of which have only served to make the modern ego dangerously fragile. Ignore the necessary myth of the Earth Mother for too long, and sacred matter will become demonic matter. Split the psyche too absolutely and what results, Jung believed, is the dark side of the splitting of matter in nuclear fission.

So Jung aims to re-orient the modern map of the psyche by re-balancing the creation myths in his writing. His methods are various. He tries to domesticate the creation myths as eros and logos potentials in the psyche. He also seeks to net the Mother Goddess as synchronicity, allowing nature to express "herself" outside Sky Father causality. In a parallel move, he asserts the presence of the feminine, body, and sexuality in the sacred or divine Self.

Jung wanted to bring Sky Father into a forgiving relationship with Earth Mother. I will end this book by looking at some of the directions suggested by this hugely ambitious cultural project. Does Jung represent a transition into a new scientific paradigm for the twenty-first century? How is post-Jungian thinking taking these powerful insights forward?

Paradigm Shifts: Emergence, Complexity, and Creativity

The Holistic Paradigm and the Creative Continuum

In Chapter 5, we looked at Jung in relation to scientific paradigms, those frameworks that shape the project of scientific enquiry. In *The Structure of Scientific Revolutions*, Thomas S. Kuhn described the two main characteristics of these powerful narratives:[17] a paradigm should be effective enough to attract adherents away from competing models; and it must remain open ended enough to allow freedom for future research.

Scientific paradigms are familiar because of their resemblance to what Jung meant by myths. In particular, the three main paradigms of the history of Western science—Aristotelian, Newtonian/reductive, and holistic—resemble combinations of the two creation myths of consciousness outlined above. For example, the Newtonian scientific paradigm is closely allied to Sky Father consciousness in its insistence upon dividing up knowledge into discrete components. In turn, the holistic paradigm now emerging seems to re-engineer Earth Mother connectivity in the portrayal of reality as an interconnected web of Being. Holism, arguably, is a necessary expansion of consciousness (by an embrace of the Other) under the aegis of Earth Mother animism and connectedness. It seeks to mend the fractures in the psyche arising from the extremes of Newtonian reductionism and the Baconian scientific method—two scientific principles that focused upon and refined the separation of subject and object.

Jung's late works evoke the new holistic paradigm when topics such as synchronicity, the role of eros in the psyche, and quantum physics lead him to posit a continuum, not a separation, between psyche and cosmos. The essential qualities of the holistic paradigm include the vital assertion that the world is an interconnected, inter-dependent whole, and thus the division between subject and object cannot hold. It follows that reality cannot be observed from *outside*, that we are always already *inside* what we look on. Complete objectivity is impossible, and the knower always colors what is to be known.

Also native to the holistic paradigm is the notion that time and space are multi-directional. Nature/cosmos can no longer be considered a soulless mechanism. Indeed, one of the best known emblems of the holistic paradigm is James Lovelock's Gaia hypothesis,[18] which directly invokes Earth Mother consciousness-through-connection by employing one of her ancient names. His theory is of a planet where living and apparently non-living elements combine to create conditions most suitable for life.

Three aspects of the holistic paradigm are significant in regarding Jung in a twenty-first century context: *chaos theory*, developed in the 1970s, and its successors in the new concepts of *complexity* and *emergence*.

Chaos theory is perhaps not well named: it does not signify a total lack of order. Rather, chaos theory recognizes a new *kind* of order in nature. Previously, order was thought to be of two types: either an entity possessed order in a steady state, or it moved from order to disorder and back to the previous order, known as "periodic return." So-called "chaos" represents the discovery of *spiral order*, the notion of a living process of patterning that produces new forms of order differing from past states. Hence the pictures of fractals which are often used to image "chaos." (Suggestively, the human heart has been discovered to follow such a "chaotic" pattern in its physical structure.)

"Complexity science" developed from chaos theory, and focuses on living biological nature.[19] Whereas the Newtonian paradigm *isolates* its objects of study, complexity, as its name suggests, looks at incredibly complex, inter-dependent *wholes*. Indeed, holism inhabits complexity science in the sense that these whole systems, known as "complex adaptive systems" (CAS), are greater than the sum of their parts. The "whole" is something *more* that just a gathering of individual entities. This means that any CAS has potency and effect that cannot be accounted for by Newtonian reductionism. For example, complex adaptive systems arise when simpler systems interact and *learn from their inter-dependence*. All parts of the CAS have a role to play, and the *network* structure is vital. The foregrounding of the supreme importance of the network points to what is arguably a new vision of the Earth Mother goddess, who is present also in that technological, human-made complex adaptive system, the World Wide Web (see below).

Chaotic systems do not learn; complex adaptive systems do. Complexity arises at the edge of the chaotic realm of nature; bios complexity *emerges* out of chaos patterning.[20] *Emergence* is the word being used to describe how something new and meaningful arises from this interaction of complex collectives. For complex adaptive systems are open-ended, implicating the ongoing evolution of ever greater and deeper complexity (an example from nature is birds in flight). However, complexity and emergence are also ways of conceptualizing the ongoing creativity of a whole ecosystem. Jungians such as Joe Cambray have even theorized that synchronicity can be understood holistically as emergence.[21]

Jung anticipated and embraced holism in a number of ways. His emphasis on teleology—where an event is "going," rather than where it comes from—draws on an Aristotelian view of nature as purposeful. His belief in the creativity of the unconscious also anticipates chaos theory, complexity, and the ever-new forms of order produced by emergence. And he knew that, when it comes to the psyche, the observer always "informs" what is observed.

Even Jung's insistence upon the creativity that comes with openness to the Other is now echoed by complexity science, which is coming to regard creativity as foundational to life itself. Wendy Wheeler, in *The Whole Creature*, makes a fascinating link between complexity's creativity in nature and human society. Two points are crucial to her argument. In the first place, the biosphere itself uses a kind of language in the way it develops complexity through the passing on of information; it *communicates, learns,* and *adapts*. Secondly, human language is not only made up of *words*. We use a truly *complex* range of bodily, paralinguistic signification that, if we follow Darwin as Wheeler does, must predate the invention of words. Interestingly, for Jungians, Wheeler believes that we are part of nature's complexity, part of the emergence of new forms, which we call "culture."

This vision embraces the individual rather than bypasses him or her. What Wheeler calls "tacit creaturely knowledge" is our learning from the Other at the borderline of chaos:

> Tacit knowledge is creaturely skilful phenomenological knowledge. Human creatures know they have it, and exult in its expression (as skilful being in the world), and in wondrous reflection upon this knowledge—which cannot be put into words, but which is experienced in all creative artisanship and art, and in creative and skilful living generally. This is language as semiosis which is not reducible to words, but which is embodied in acts.[22]

Such "creaturely knowledge" is *learning from what Jung called the unconscious.* Like Wheeler, Jung saw the unconscious as both embodied and encultured, so his notion of individuation—the lifelong forging of a relationship to the unconscious for the sake of psychic health—is also human participation in the creativity of nature.

Both Wheeler and Jung embrace this notion of reality and science as intrinsically creative; complexity science puts creativity and ethics at its heart. A vision of interdependence between complex adaptive systems of human culture, psyche, and nature, means that generating an ethical relation to the Other is at the heart of survival. Humans are creatures who need the Other(s) to be whole.

Jung and Re-Connecting to Nature and Cosmos

Two more perspectives on a twenty-first century reconnection with nature are worth considering here, in both of which the Jungian legacy is augmented by, and in turn expands, the holistic paradigm. Jerome Bernstein, in *Living in the Borderland*,[23] has reexamined Jung's accounts of his travels among Native Americans (see Chapter 2). But in his far more nuanced comparative cultural study, Bernstein shows the "emergence" in the Western psyche of disorders that can be best understood through a paradigm about our connection with nature like that of the American Navajo.

As a Jungian analyst, Bernstein noticed that some patients were coming to him with distress that they refused to attribute to personal or even human events. Rather, these patients felt so connected to the suffering of nature itself that the pain of cows in a truck or of trees being cut down became *their* pain. These patients are "living in the borderland," where psyche has a real, textured bond to nature.

Like Wheeler, Bernstein understands these phenomena by drawing on a narrative of evolution. Once, prior to a Sky Father understanding of Genesis which cut us off from nature, we all lived in the borderland. Modernity made gains for the Western psyche by focusing on increasing ego consciousness. Now, however, the imbalance severing us from the Other—from nature, the unconscious, other people—must be redressed. "Borderland" patients are pioneers; they show the way psyche needs to evolve if we are to avoid destroying ourselves.

By drawing upon the culture of the Navajo as one founded on reverence for the psychic connection with nature, Bernstein is also able to enrich and fortify Jung's notion of the healing powers of story. The Navajo do not distinguish between sickness of mind and body, because they have a holistic vision of the person in the cosmos. Sickness means loss of the life-giving bond to in-spirited nature. Such pain is not individual and personal; it is rather a tear in the fabric of the cosmos. So the bond to nature must be restored by means of the "complex" of mythical stories. These stories heal through their being enacted, *lived*. They are integrated into body and spirit by means of rituals that re-make the whole web of Being.

By contrast, the modern patient visiting an analyst has no such web of stories, so first of all, the pain needs to be understood through the creation in therapy of a narrative that can contain it. This is the "trauma story." Such a story may or may not recount events that have factually occurred, but the important point is that it captures and expresses the essence of the trauma. But then there is a further task.

Again through analysis, a new "origin story" can be generated. This is slightly paradoxical—an origin story that is not about literal beginnings! But it *is* about re-birth. The new origin story gives new meaning in the holistic sense of re-connecting the person to a reciprocal, living, animated cosmos. Since Westerners have been traumatically severed from nature by the over-privileging of the rational ego, what is needed is a *new* origin story that allows us to be re-born from the Earth Mother as well as from the Sky Father. The new origin story enables the person to recognize that they are part of the great web of complexity and emergent processes that make up nature and culture.

Astrologer Richard Tarnas is certainly seeking a new origin story for modernity in *Cosmos and Psyche*.[24] An intriguing project of cultural recovery, Tarnas begins with Plato's theory of perfect invisible Forms that provide the underlying order for cosmos and humanity. Plato's notion ultimately appeared too rigid to last unchallenged, but the sense of intuitive archetypal order in the cosmos continued in astrology. Jung was interested in how astrological symbolism remained part of the Western heritage of religious symbols, but Bernstein goes one step further than Jung in confidently asserting the psychic connection to nature. Similarly, Tarnas steps forward to propose that astrology links the cosmos to the psyche through a common archetypal dimension.

Here the holistic paradigm is exemplified in the revelation of a sentient, meaningful cosmos in which time is qualitative as well as quantitative, and in which history has an archetypal, cosmic reality. Just as holism proposes that we affect what we purport to merely observe, and as Bernstein believes that we need to evolve a "borderland consciousness" in order to survive, so Tarnas argues for the value of astrology:

> [Understanding] unconscious archetypal dynamics that coincide with planetary cycles and alignments, both in individual lives and in the historical process, can play a crucial role in the positive unfolding of our collective future.[25]

Other new works inspired by Jung continue to open up paths into the holistic paradigm. I will look briefly at the philosophy of phenomenology, which in turn contributes to a new kind of learning. I will then turn to a new understanding of matter in technology, and ultimately to our new digital reality as manifested in the internet.

New Psychology, New World View: Jung and Phenomenology

I am greatly indebted to the work of Roger Brooke for this section. His book, *Jung and Phenomenology*, and his edited essay collection, *Pathways into the Jungian World*, are indispensable and comprehensive.[26]

Phenomenology was first developed by philosopher Edmund Husserl as a way of looking at "things in themselves," without a pre-structuring theory or idea—without even our common assumption that we are subjects divided off from objects. Phenomenology is, therefore, an attempt to live the holistic paradigm, most intensely. For to be truly phenomenological is to realize oneself as an embodied mind, and to do that is to "bracket off" whatever obscures the reality of the Other in our living perception. Is it possible to interrogate a phenomenon on its own terms and not only on ours? Phenomenology takes up the challenge.

Jung claimed to be phenomenological in his attempts to investigate the psyche on its own terms. He was most successful, Brooke shows, when dealing with religious images and experiences, which he insisted be treated as authentic psychic material and the integrity of the image respected as it develops in the psyche. Brooke puts it this way:

> This fundamental dialectic (the ground of the hermeneutic circle) means that the description of the meaning of the phenomena has an interpretative moment that intuitively reaches through individual occurrences to their phenomenological heart or "structure."[27]

Yet despite Jung's genuine focus on psychic phenomena and on allowing that focus to generate meaning, Brooke shows that he was no true phenomenologist. He does not bracket off his assumptions successfully, often assuming a subject/object division that perpetuates the dualisms of inside/outside, mind/body, and subject/world that phenomenology explicitly disavows.

This is, however, another case where Jung's developing holism leads him toward the sort of new paradigm constituted by phenomenology. The Jung who proposed an archetypal dimension to the cosmos itself is apparent most overtly in his theory of synchronicity, in which he relies upon a phenomenological mode of perceiving the growth of meaning through the living connection of self and sentient other.

I would like to propose that Jung is also a phenomenologist in another key aspect: his *writing*. Jung's writing is, in holistic terms, a *complex adaptive system* that comes alive when *realized* (made real) in the psyche of the reader. It is more of a complex adaptive system than most writing because Jung treated writing phenomenologically, as rhetoric. Jung develops his notion of the rhetorical psyche most evidently in "On the Nature of the Psyche."[28]

Writing like this knows itself as psychic creativity. "On the Nature of the Psyche" is not *about* the psyche, it *enacts it*—a rhetorical strategy that spirals outward like a chaotic system giving rise to ever-new, emergent forms of order. These *emerging forms of order* are the creative blooming of Jung's visions of psyche and cosmos. The writing generates meanings through the web-like growth of its rhetoric, a complex system *adapting* to the mind of the reader. Jung uses writing as *revelation* of psyche; what begins as description becomes an unfolding of the creative self. My book, *Jung as a Writer*, shows in detail how this particular essay of Jung's functions as phenomenological rhetoric.[29]

If Jung was in some ways incorporating holism and phenomenology into his writing, what implications might this hold for the question of learning? The recent publication of *The Wounded Researcher*, by depth psychologist and phenomenologist Robert Romanyshyn, is a successful pathway toward a new holistic vision of education.[30] How might the new paradigm of one-ness with cosmos and nature, based on our reevaluation of the role of the unconscious, show itself in scholarship? After all, Western universities are segregated into disciplines, a structure and philosophy built on the Newtonian paradigm of division and separation.

Like Jung, Romanyshyn begins with our wounds, and finds in them the sources of new being. His book is a fundamental challenge to scholarship as it has developed in modernity.

Holistic Learning

All those who do psychological research are wounded because of the ultimate failure of our tools, methods, language, and even our thinking. They fail because of what Jung knew most intimately through his work: that what is most significant, most *real*, the unconscious psyche, cannot be captured alive.

Our depths, the depths of being and world, which Romanyshyn refers to as the soul, cannot fully be known. Psychological research that does not acknowledge this truth, along with the *vitality* it implies, is research without soul. In perfecting only the rational tools of the ego, modernity has suffered from soul-less psychological research, and has thereby generated ego inflation. An inflated ego can acknowledge no Other; hence, as Jung argued, soul-less research treats nature as an object.

Romanyshyn demonstrates that, just as all research is inevitably suffused with the unconscious psyche (for, invoked or not, the unconscious is always present), there is also a soul *of* research. The first step in honoring this soul is to recognize that there is a fundamental wound in our work: the gap between our language and the subtle reality which our efforts aim to examine.

Romanyshyn offers a poetics of psychological research, exploring the pregnant "gap" between language and substance of meaning. Myth is drawn into academic pursuit, only to reveal that it was present all the time. In one resonant chapter, Romanyshyn examines the experience of the researcher in relation to the myth of Orpheus and Eurydice. The researcher is the suffering poet, deeply wounded by the separation from his soul, his beloved Other, that is, the subject of his psychological research. So he embarks on a journey in order to find "her," downwards and inwards to the underworld of psyche. What is "found" or "uncovered" is brought back from the inner depths, and yet research writing must *necessarily* fail to encompass the deep psyche. The researcher ultimately climbs out of the underworld alone, for the knowledge revealed by research (Eurydice) must be released, set free to be *itself* and not what the researcher might desire it to be.

Like Orpheus, however, whose head continues singing even after it is cut off from his body, the researcher also "sings," articulating the research in writing nourished by the imagination of the underworld and the wholeness of the body, but severed from this bodily and imaginal wholeness *by the act of writing itself.* In order to put his deep re-search into words, the researcher sacrifices, with pain and reverence, many dimensions and aspects of the Other that were discovered in the process.

Orpheus' descent to the underworld and the subsequent loss of Eurydice teaches us that we cannot possess what we love. Likewise for the researcher, knowledge cannot become a mere possession of the ego; we bring back only Eurydice's echo.

There is a much more in *The Wounded Researcher*, and the book certainly provides sustenance for the whole self in the activity of scholarly research. For example, Romanyshyn uncovers the presence of Hermes as the mythological figure of the "gap" in language, and his alchemical hermeneutics invokes the unconscious of both the reader and the work itself in the interpretative process. The "hermeneutic circle" becomes a spiral, as I suggested of Jung's own writing in Chapter 2, above.

The Wounded Researcher is part of a new holism of culture, for it attempts to restore imagination and eros to the world of learning. Imagination and eros bless our connections to the Other as a *source* of ethical knowledge. Ultimately, and far more explicitly than Jung, Romanyshyn, Brooke, and the phenomenologists aim to reconcile eros and logos. They try to bring Earth Mother and Sky Father into co-operation and love.

The In-spired Matter of Technology
Lee Worth Bailey's *The Enchantments of Technology*[31] is an important book which proposes a new "alchemy" in its exploration of matter as *animated*. Modern technology, Bailey demonstrates, has been forged from our own myths, passions, dreams, unconscious monsters, and desires. Far from modernity's having renounced myth, Bailey asserts that myth has found a profound home in technology. Here he echoes Jung in *Aion*, who quotes the Gnostic myth of God's descending into matter.[32] For Jung, as we have shown, this myth traces the descent of the sacred into matter, until materialism became modernity's new god.

Bailey, too, uses a phenomenological approach. This challenge to the subject/object distinction pierces through the apparent disenchantment of material reality in modernity to show what it actually incarnates:

There is no technical thought without enchantment because technological culture is teeming with dreams, visions, hopes, goals, expectations, and imaginative premises.[33]

Crucially, Bailey points to Plato's assumption of a relation between logos (rationality) and mythos (knowledge through story, imagination), which

Christianity tried hard to pry apart; but through approaches such as those of phenomenology and Jung, eros and logos can rediscover a being-in-relationship. In a chapter entitled "The Bottomless Subject," Bailey suggests that the long Western construct that keeps reason separate from body and desire can be overcome. Reason and desire can be properly reunited because the subject is "bottomless," because reason is organically connected to body and to a great well of collective desires and enchantments.

Hence technology's rational element is not separable from, nor wholly other to, a body of irrational creative fantasy. In this psychic reality, metaphors operate as fishing hooks to catch powerful expressions of soul afloat in the collective realm, such that, for example, the Golden Gate Bridge in San Francisco takes up a transcendent imaginal existence, *bridging* individual and collective, making of its *matter* a *spiritual* phenomenon.

Particularly fascinating is Bailey's historical analysis of the technologies of the camera obscura and magic lantern, for these shaped our Western notion of subjectivity through projection. A camera obscura was a device used by Renaissance painters to help them produce the effect of "perspective" in their works, while the magic lantern projected images onto a screen for entertainment. Although these are merely explicable forms of technology, they also came to embody beliefs about the human mind. Revelations of the psyche, such devices also function as enchanting metaphors that generate, in a sort of feedback-loop, their own versions of human knowledge.

Modernity has modeled its conception of thought on the magic lantern: the skull is conceived as a screen, upon which the mind *projects* its images of the world. Even Jungian psychology tells us that we *project* our subjective feelings onto the real world, and says we must "withdraw" those projections. In Bailey's persuasive analysis, such a model is far from a necessary truth about how the psyche actually works.

Enchantment, as the wisdom of fairy tales shows, is dangerous, and the modern world is dangerously unconscious of the dark fantasies it has incarnated in technological "progress." Yet perhaps working with what have now come to recognize as *enchanting, enchanted* matter could enable us to creatively splice together new and ancient forms of consciousness. Bailey argues that this occurred for the American astronauts in space, endowing them with a sense of the numinosity of the earth, enabling them to blend the pinnacle of modernity's rational science with an embodied *imaginative* vision.

Conclusion: The Fisher King and the Net of the World Wide Web

In his book, *The Sunken Quest, The Wasted Fisher, The Pregnant Fish*, Ronald Schenk writes that Jung, at his phenomenological best, urges a conjoining of the fundamental dualism of Western thought,[34] that founding division (sponsored by the two creation myths) between form and matter.[35] His powerful argument is for a Jung liberated by his own inclinations toward holism and its phenomenological methods. Such a twenty-first century Jung deconstructs his own frequent motif of fishing or fish. Let us pause for a moment at Jung fishing!

In writing of alchemy, for example, Jung often used the fisherman as metaphor for the ego trying to hook nourishment from the unconscious. Dreams of fish signify the slippery elusive nature of unconscious images. Round fish are mandala forms. Glowing fish eyes image the archetypes in the darkness of the unconscious. A fish, of course, signifies Christ in ancient symbolism, and the two fish which indicate Pisces alert us to the duality of the Self, reminding us that Jung's Christ has a dark brother whom modern Christianity forgot.

Yet all these piscatorial images are also telling an important story of the observer and the observed. Our metaphors encode worldviews. The fisherman looks at the water and sees the *separate* eyes of the fish looking back at him. T.S. Eliot ended his mythical poem about modernity, "The Wasteland," with a fisherman.[36] Thus a long poem, exemplifying the notion of modern fragmentation, ends in a moment of calm, even peace. Less optimistic than Jung, we do not know if Eliot's fisherman is successful in catching either a fish or Christ; he is merely hopeful. Jung, however, suggests that the alchemical fisherman has such an imaginative relationship with the fish that he might even change places with him! Until he incorporates the fish bodily, Eliot and Jung's men and fish are stuck looking at each other in the subject/object position. Yet Jung, sometimes unknown even to himself, was trawling deeply for holism in his researches, and Schenk has recognized and revealed it.

We have found with Jung that self has moved from noun to verb, from defining or declaring to gathering and questioning. Am I the fisher reeling in or reeling about? Baiting or hooked myself? The fish in labor or the fetus emerging, or the doctor groping? Am I the infant raging or the rabbit charred? Am I author or rumor? Am I calling on the spirits of Jung or Eliot to drop in on us, or a man on stage dropping names?[37]

The World Wide Web: *The Way North,* by Joel Weishaus

Digital literary art, of which Joel Weishaus is one of the pioneers, is *text as text-ure*. By "text-ure," I mean to suggest signs or images on the World Wide Web that are crafted to emphasize their *material mystery*. Text-ure draws attention to the metaphors of "net" and "web" that haunt our screens, embodying in art Earth Mother matter as dreaming psyche. It is an art form forging new relationships with audience, matter, culture, nature, and cosmos. A resonant example, born and living happily on the web, is Weishaus' *The Way North.*[38] This work beautifully exemplifies Jung's own intuitive sense of the need for a new animism, for listening to the many voices of soul, body, and nature.

An introductory page evokes the ancient artistic roots of this new art form, suggesting that these artistic forebears found ways of living with and loving what we would regard as a particularly cruel manifestation of our Other, nature:

> During the last ice age *Homo Sapiens* were tested as to whether they could survive extreme climatic conditions. Not only did our ancestors survive, they generated an art that has never been surpassed on the scale of its multimedia daring.[39]

The Way North is a tribute to and ritual evocation of shamanic art. These prehistoric multimedia artists used stone, sound, chant, painting, story, and ritual. Echoing them, Weishaus' art incorporates photographs of ice and stone cairns, and includes fragments of poetry, sounds, and autobiographical storytelling, as well as history and myth from the sagas of Norse warriors to the use of the North by the modern military.

The text also weaves in quotations from the long history of Western culture's fascination with the North. This mysterious land has been regarded as a region beyond conquest, seeming to resist the anti-nature culture of the West. Nor does *The Way North* shy from depicting the polluting footprint of modernity, tracing the loss by global warming of nature's long culturing of the North in its immanence, its intrinsic spirituality. Pollution causing the melting of ice caps is contamination, through human greed and ignorance, of non-human nature's artistry. Weishaus shows modernity's destructiveness and blind incomprehension of the Other.

In contrast to modernity's culture of dominance, *The Way North* is, as its name tells us, a *way*—a direction for the imagination. The text is text-ure because it is art as body of (Earth M)other, not as the constructed image of some separate reality (which would be Sky Father art). Text-ure is not *re*-presentation, it is action. It is art *which generates being in imagination*; it does not produce a secondary account of an apparently separate "reality." *The Way North* is a multiplicitous gathering of the psyche from all its homes. Psyche dwells in bodily senses, in the personal soul (fragmentary intimacies shared) and the impersonal soul (love poems), in history, and in culture. All of (the many parts of) us are gathered into a relationship with and through this art-matter.

I say "art-matter" because digital literary art is born from deep in the very matter, the mattering, of the World Wide Web. We *know* that the internet is codes and pulses of light, yet we still see it as evocative words, images, designs, and sounds. Such digital literary art opens us to aware-ness of the reciprocal pulses of energy that make up the human body and signal its place in the cosmos.

The Earth Mother sponsors *The Way North* because it is art of her *web of complete Being*. Such creative work recasts the human relation to nature as a desire for love. In order to truly find the goddess again, modernity needs to understand the extent of our loss of humanness through our inhuman treatment of the earth.

We have to look beyond the culture we have directly inherited, as Jung did, and as Weishaus does here (in his case, toward shamans and the internet), in order to fully comprehend the horror and blankness we have achieved. The West has called down its own darkness by refusing the imaginative challenge of North. Instead we pollute it, treating its other-ness as dead matter.

Jung saw that in alchemy, North was the abode of hell because it embodied the paradox of a dark/light divine. It incarnated the Otherness of monotheism, its dark side, in an imagined fire burning in the ice. Alchemy incarnated a strong presence of Earth Mother in Western culture, but this gradually became obscured. For Jung's North, the North Pole is a cardinal point, an orientation, a source of magnetism for navigation. North is not just a metaphor for the psyche. Rather, the matter of psyche and the matters of world *matter* because they are not separable. As *The Way North* shows, what we do to the North, we do to ourselves.

Weishaus does not directly call his North "hell." For Jung, the identification of North with hell means that North/hell is a stimulus for the work of the imagination. If we regard hell from the Sky Father perspective, as a *separate* realm in a steady state, hell is the dust-bin of the Sky Father god for the imperfect human soul. Such definitive damnation, however, is not the alchemical way. Hell has also to be seen from the Earth Mother perspective as an integral part of the living psyche, a necessary and terrible dimension of the imagination.

To Jung and the alchemists, we cannot just ignore such hellish places, the dark matter of the divine. Hell must be faced, endured, and visited as an underworld. The psyche sends us to visit hell even if we have to leave it without our Eurydice, our heart's desire. Hell may be a spatial term: hell as a place. It may be a period of time. Or it may be death, and the fear of death. All modes of hell have to be *in-corporated* into the psyche. Alchemy points us in that direction. *The Way North*, likewise, tells us that we must embrace hellish latitudes. We should imaginatively incarnate those infernal regions in order to stop hurting ourselves by harming nature. In experiencing the ritual that *The Way North* provides for consciousness, we find *art as a healing alchemy.*

For such art, the cosmos is sentient, reciprocal, and delicate. It emphasizes immanence without being wholly immanent, for that would be to dissolve consciousness rather than re-make it. All of us are in a relationship between the Sky Father (art as wholly separate, a discrete object) and Earth Mother (art as an extension of the creativity of nature).

To be human is to retain some of the Sky Father sense of Otherness-to-nature. Weishaus inspires because *The Way North* is in-spirited by intimations of transcendence. Yet these are never allowed to break away from his work's loving immanence in Earth Mother's creative nature. *The Way North* is a re-weaving of Western consciousness. Such work brings us home, at last.

So we end a book on Jung with an evocation of new web-based consciousness. The twenty-first century challenges us to save ourselves by re-making our relationship to the planet. Jung's psychology is one form of writing that can be a thread leading out of dark places, and weaving new ones.

FURTHER READING

Lee Worth Bailey, *The Enchantments of Technology* (Urbana and Chicago: University of Chicago Press, 2005).
   A major work that dispels our modern illusion of living in a technological world created by reason. Bailey uncovers the passion and myth driving our love of machines.

John Beebe, "The Anima in Film," in Christopher Hauke and Ian Alister, eds., *Jung and Film* (London and New York: Routledge, 2001), pp. 208-225.
   A superb analysis of the erotic power of certain female stars.

Jerome S. Bernstein, *Living in the Borderland: The Evolution of Consciousness and the Challenge of Healing Trauma* (London and New York: Routledge, 2005).
   Bernstein takes Jung's work a stage further, proposing an important new evolutionary shift for human consciousness: rejoining nature. This book is radical and prophetic.

Roger Brooke, *Jung and Phenomenology* (London and New York: Routledge, 1993).
Roger Brooke, ed., *Pathways into the Jungian World: Phenomenology and Analytical Psychology* (London and New York: Routledge, 2000).
   Brooke is an expert communicator on the demanding topic of phenomenology.

Joseph Cambray, "Synchronicity as Emergence," in Joseph Cambray and Linda Carter, eds., *Analytical Psychology: Contemporary Perspectives in Jungian Analysis* (London and New York: Brunner-Routledge, 2004), pp. 223-248.
   Cambray cogently makes the case for Jung having pioneered certain aspects of emergence science.

Angela Connolly, "Jung in the Twilight Zone: The Psychological Functions of the Horror Film," in Susan Rowland, ed., *Psyche and the Arts* (London and New York: Routledge, 2008), pp. 128-138.
A detailed analysis of horror film, with lots of examples.

Jacques Derrida, *Of Grammatology*, trans. Gayatri Chakravorty Spivak, (Baltimore, MD: Johns Hopkins University Press, 1977).
It is worth persevering with this early work of deconstruction, which has a real affinity with Jungian ideas.

T.S. Eliot, "The Wasteland," in Margaret Ferguson, Mary Jo Salter and Jon Stallworthy, eds., *The Norton Anthology of Poetry* (New York and London: W.W. Norton, 1922/2005).

Christopher Hauke, *Jung and the Postmodern: The Interpretation of Realities* (London and New York: Routledge, 2000).
A very good starting place for exploring the relation between Jung and postmodern philosophy. The affinities are startling.

Raya Jones, *Jung, Psychology, Postmodernity* (London and New York: Routledge, 2007).
A persuasive and provocative reading of Jung in a philosophical and psychological context.

Paul Kugler, *Raids on the Unthinkable: Freudian and Jungian Psychoanalyses* (New Orleans: Spring Journal Books, 2005).
By applying poststructuralist thinking to depth psychology, Kugler makes powerful arguments about psychoanalysis, language, and the perception of reality.

Thomas Kuhn, *The Structure of Scientific Revolutions* (Chicago: University Chicago Press, 1962).

David A. Leeming, Kathryn Madden and Stanton Marlan, eds., *Encyclopedia of Psychology and Religion* (Springer, http://www.springer.com/psychology/psychology+general/book/978-0-387-71802-6, 2010)

James Lovelock, *Gaia: A New Look at Life on Earth* (Oxford: Oxford University Press, 1979/2000).

David L. Miller, *Hells and Holy Ghosts: A Theopoetics of Christian Belief* (New Orleans: Spring Journal Books, 2004).
Miller offers a powerful psychological and revisionary understanding of hell.

Robert Romanyshyn, *The Wounded Researcher: Research with Soul in Mind* (New Orleans: Spring Journal Books, 2007).
Romanyshyn has produced a magnificent revision of traditional academic research methodologies, bringing into the process crucial aspects of the psyche hitherto excluded.

Ferdinand de Saussure, extract from *Course in General Linguistics* (1916), in Julie Rivkin and Michael Ryan, eds., *Literary Theory: An Anthology* (Oxford: Blackwell, 2004), pp. 59-71.

Ronald Schenk, *The Sunken Quest, The Wasted Fisher, The Pregnant Fish* (Wilmette, IL: Chiron, 2001).
An imaginative and intelligent and empathetic reading of Jung for the new age.

Richard Tarnas, *Cosmos and Psyche: Intimations of a New World View* (New York: Viking, 2006).
In a striking blend of psychology and astrology, Tarnas presents a detailed historical case for the new holistic paradigm.

Joel Weishaus, *The Way North* (http://www.cddc.vt.edu/host/weishaus/htm).
A pioneer of digital literary art, Weishaus is a poet for an age needing a new relationship between its founding creation myths in order to re-make consciousness.

Wendy Wheeler, *The Whole Creature: Complexity, Biosemiotics, and the Evolution of Culture* (London: Laurence & Wishart, 2006).

Although not a Jungian, Wheeler struggles with integrity to bring creativity, ethics, and language into a nature-culture continuum.

Glossary

Words in **bold** are Jungian terms included in this Glossary.

It is important to note that there are a number of gendered binaries in Jungian terminology, such as **anima/animus** and **Logos/Eros**. Jung himself often held rather literalistic ideas about these binaries, as reflected in the Glossary below. The reader is asked to bear in mind, however, that contemporary Jungian analytic theory and practice have extended such concepts and consequently treat archetypal binaries as equally available to both genders.

Active Imagination

This is the term Jung gave to his therapeutic method of having a patient spontaneously fantasize upon an image, usually a **dream** image, although Jung argued that cultural, mythical, or artistic images could also be used as starting points. Active imagination surrenders conscious direction of fantasies to "the Other," that is, the **unconscious**. **Unconscious** material is thereby brought into **consciousness**, and **individuation** is promoted.

Alchemy

Alchemy was more than the doomed and greedy attempt to turn lead into gold. It also relied upon philosophical and religious beliefs that held that mind, matter, and divine spirit existed in a continuum. Gold and lead, for example, were the material aspects of substances that were equally psychological and divine, and the work of the alchemist was to refine and release the soul from its incarceration in base matter. In alchemy, the forerunner of modern materialist chemistry, mental and spiritual work still existed alongside actual chemical operations.

Alchemy (Jungian)

Alchemy is defined by Jung as *the projection of the alchemist's psychic contents*, specifically of the **individuation** process, *upon the activities of* *physical matter*. He interpreted alchemical texts as demonstrating that alchemists were in fact *unwitting self-analysts*. Alchemists developed **symbols**, which Jung believed enabled psychological transformations (similar to the role of **dreams** in his psychological method). In his view, alchemists used chemistry and symbolic language to stimulate their own **individuation**, so that they could reach the "gold" of union with the divine, or the **archetype** of the **Self**.

Amplification

Amplification is a Jungian therapeutic technique whereby a psychic image (such as from a **dream**) is *amplified* by linking it to **mythological** motifs. This serves to render the image less personal, and so suggests something of the Otherness of the **unconscious**. Amplification consequently tends to downplay questions of the patient's personal history.

Anima

According to Jung, the anima is the **archetype** of the feminine in the **unconscious** of a man. In that this notion locates a feminine mode in the subjectivity of the masculine gender, denoting a bisexual **unconscious**, it is a helpful concept. However, Jung at times models female subjectivity on his *own* **unconscious** anima, leading him to designate women as "more unconscious" than men.

Animus

The animus is the **archetype** of masculinity in the **unconscious** of a woman. As with the **anima**, this characterization need not lock Jungian theory into perpetual gender opposition, since the **unconscious** is a realm in which nothing can be securely known or fixed, and contains androgynous **archetypes**. Masculinity is rather one of a series of types of Otherness for the psyche of a woman.

Archetypes

Archetypes are inherited structuring patterns in the **unconscious**, with potentials for meaning formation. They are unrepresentable in themselves, becoming evident only in their manifest derivatives, **archetypal images**. Archetypes are containers of opposites and so are androgynous, equally capable of manifesting themselves as either gender, or even as non-human forms. **Body** and culture influence the content of **archetypal images**, but do not govern them because archetypes are the structuring principles of an *autonomous* psyche. Archetypes are not inherited ideas or images.

Archetypal Images

Archetypal images are the visible representations of **archetypes**. A single image can never account for the multifarious potential of the **archetype**, which is why archetypal images are always provisional and partial images of a greater unrepresentable complexity. Crucially, archetypal imagery is always cultural and historical as well as psychic, numinous, and creative, drawing its *representative material* from culture and its *structuring energy* from the **archetype**.

Body

The Jungian notion of the body is of both an unknowable entity separated from the psyche, and something that is vitally connected to the psyche. Indeed, **archetypes** are rooted in the body as well as having a transcendent spiritual dimension. The body cannot *control* signification, but does *influence* it. For example, sexuality is a bodily function that can liberate archetypal energies. A sexual act has its bodily integrity, yet it may simultaneously become a rite, entering a numinous dimension that alchemists (and Jung after them) called a "sacred marriage."

Collective Unconscious

The collective **unconscious** is the common inheritance of **archetypes** that all human beings share. How the **archetypes** are then manifested as **archetypal images** will depend upon the particular culture and history of any individual.

Consciousness

Consciousness is that part of the psyche realized by the **ego**. It is the *known* and *knowable* about every human person. For Jung, psychic health requires that consciousness be in touch with healing **unconscious** powers through **individuation**. One way to be in contact with the **unconscious** is the enjoyment of art.

Counter-transference
This refers to the tendency for the **unconscious** contents of the analyst to get projected onto the patient in analysis. Jung was one of the first to realize the importance of this phenomenon.

Dreams
Unlike the Freudian usage, dreams to a Jungian are spontaneous expressions or communications from a superior part of the human mind. They are not derivative of **ego** concerns or necessarily about sexuality (unless they belong to the trivial class of dreams derived from the residue of the previous day). Dream images are not a secondary but rather a *primary* form of reality, and must not be "translated" into the mode of the **ego**, into mere words. Jung believed something very similar about art: that it could offer a primary mode of expression of the **unconscious**, provided that it fell into the category of **visionary art**, in which the artist is possessed by the archetypal imagination.

Ego
The ego is the centre of **consciousness** concerned with the sense of a personal identity, the maintenance of personality, and the sense of continuity over time. However, Jung considered the ego as less than the whole personality, and saw it as constantly interacting with more significant archetypal forces in the **unconscious**. Jung tended to equate the ego with **consciousness** in his writings.

Enantiodromia
This term expresses a core Jungian insight: that in the psyche, things have the habit of turning into their own opposite. The emergence of opposites in the **unconscious** is a frequent characteristic of **individuation**.

Eros
Eros is another of Jung's concepts based upon gendered opposites; its Other is **logos**. Eros stands for psychic capacities of relatedness and feeling, with **logos** as a motif of spiritual meaning and reason. Jung aligned feminine **consciousness** with eros and masculine subjectivity with **logos**. Since the **anima** and **animus** carry eros and **logos** qualities in the

unconscious, this means that males tend to have underdeveloped qualities of relating, while females to be inferior in "thinking" and rational argument. The consequences for Jung's views on gender are profound.

God–Image

The Jungian **archetype** of the **Self** is frequently represented by a divine figure or god-image in the psyche. This is because the **unconscious** self is the goal of **individuation**, the supreme desire of the psyche, and therefore produces spontaneous divine images.

Individuation

Individuation is Jung's term for the process whereby the **ego** is brought into a relationship with the archetypal dynamics of the **unconscious**. In individuation, the **ego** is constantly made, unmade, and re-made by the goal-directed forces of the **unconscious**. Even "meaning" in the **ego** is subject to dissolution and re-constitution by the Other. For Jung, the making and appreciation of art were forms of individuation because they involve a confrontation with the Other in imagination.

Logos

A principle of mental functioning oriented toward reason, discrimination, and spiritual authority, Jung regarded logos as characteristic of masculine **consciousness**. Logos operates in a gendered binary opposite with **eros**.

Mythology and Myth

The term "mythology" conventionally refers to the stories of gods, goddesses, monsters, and divine beings that have performed a religious function in various human societies. Examples would include the mythologies of ancient Greece and Rome; Christianity, too, may be regarded as a mythology. However, to Jung, myth is rather more than this limited definition. It is also a form of language that enables participation in the unexplored—and in some sense unconquerable—territories of the mind. To Jung, myth posses a double psychic potency: it is at the same time the most authentic *representation* of the interplay of **consciousness** and the **unconscious**, and an active *intervention* shaping such inner dialogue. Myth can perform a healing function when the **unconscious** threatens mental chaos, while it is simultaneously a true expression of the mutuality of the two aspects of the psyche, **consciousness** and the **unconscious**. For Jung and Jungian literary theory, true *expression* of the psyche is privileged over conceptually-based claims to *know* it.

Oedipus Complex
Freud posited an **unconscious** structured by the male infant's repression of his sexual desires for the mother, which becomes reconfigured as forbidden. The male child's desire to continue the passionate bond to the nurturing (m)Other through his discovery of genital pleasure is interrupted by his intimation of the role of the father. At first loathing the father and desiring his removal, the child comes to fear retribution from him in the form of castration. This nascent tragedy is resolved by the child identifying with the paternal function and repressing prohibited desires for the mother, so creating a sexual **unconscious**. This dramatic process of guilt, forbidden desire, and criminal fantasy Freud called the Oedipus complex, after the Greek tragic hero.

Persona
The persona is the mask worn by the **ego** in the outer world, the way the **ego** *adapts* so as to present a coherent personality in social situations. Over-identification with the persona means that the more challenging forces from the **unconscious** are ignored. **Individuation** is a process of detaching identity from the persona in order to engage with the **unconscious**.

Personal Unconscious
The notion of the personal **unconscious** is the means by which Jung wove Freudian ideas into his own mature thought. The Jungian personal **unconscious** is equivalent to the Freudian idea of the unconscious as created by Oedipal sexual repression. For Jung, what was far more important than the personal **unconscious** was the **collective unconscious** and the **archetype**s.

Phallus

For the post-Freudian psychoanalyst Jacques Lacan, the phallus is a privileged signifier representing the cultural form of patriarchy, the imposition of the Law of the Father whereby a person enters the Symbolic Order and becomes socialized, yet is internally split in the process. Although it is not to be equated to the fleshly penis, the phallus organizes a person's gender upon entry to language and the symbolic. The phallus is what the masculine very ambivalently "has," and what the feminine must "be" for the masculine. The effect of the phallus is to make the masculine the "natural" home of power and meaning.

Psychological Art

Jung divided art into psychological and **visionary** categories. Psychological art mainly consists of **signs**, which points to what is known or knowable. It consequently expresses primarily the collective **consciousness** of a society, and consists of whatever the collective is consciously debating or concerned about. Jung felt that in some art, the artist has already done most of the psychic work for the audience—hence "psychological" art.

Religious Experience

Religious experience in Jungian theory is distinctive because, to Jung, all experience is mediated through the psyche and its structuring principles, the **archetypes**. Viewed *psychologically*, religious experience is not considered as emanating from a *separate* supernatural reality (although Jung's ideas are nevertheless often congruent with such a possibility). Religious experiences are the property of the supreme **archetype, the Self**.

Self

The Self is the supreme governing **archetype** of the **unconscious**, to which the **ego** becomes subject in **individuation**. Jung frequently described Self-images in **dreams** as circular or mandala forms, and he argued that Christ functioned as a Self-image in Christianity. What is crucial to remember is that "Self" for Jung meant the *not-known*, the *unknowable* in the psyche. The Self is to be found in the **unconscious**; in contrast with **ego**, it does not represent the conscious personality.

Shadow

The shadow is the archetypal force of reversal or undoing. Intrinsic to the idea of a compensatory relation between **ego** and **unconscious**, the shadow is that which is denied by the conscious personality. The shadow can consequently be figured as the potential for evil within everyone. Jung warned that the shadow needed to be brought into a *relationship* with conscious personality, lest repression cause it to swell in power and break out in neurosis or violence.

Signs

Jung divided images into two types: signs and **symbols**. Signs point to a known or knowable meaning. They are therefore primarily concerned with the collective **consciousness**, and are the main element of **psychological art**.

Symbols

Symbols represent Jung's second type of image; they point to what is hardly known, not yet known, or unknowable. They are therefore the chief conduit for the **collective unconscious** in **dreams** and in **visionary art**. **Archetypal images**, with their numinous quality, very often manifest as symbols.

Subtle Body

The **body** as imaged in the psyche is a Jungian "subtle body," formed by both bodily and archetypal elements. Because **archetypes** are of the **body** as well as of the non-bodily psyche, mental *representations* of the **body** are both physical *and* psychical—hence, the subtle body.

Symbolic, Jungian

Like Lacanian theory, Jungian theory also proposes a symbolic order, with crucial differences. For Jung, the **unconscious** is not determined by repression, and contains autonomous androgynous principles called **archetypes**. Jung's symbolic therefore does not necessarily repress the feminine. In the Jungian symbolic, feminine imagery can exist for itself; it is not doomed to function as a screen for masculine fantasy.

Synchronicity

Jung used this term to describe the linking of events *not* by cause and effect, *not* by time and space, but by *psychological coherence*. For example, if a total stranger were suddenly to fulfil a person's vital need for some type of idea, information, or encounter, but with no apparent explanation for the occurrence—that is synchronicity. It a key expression of Jung's notion that psyche, matter, time, and space are all fundamentally connected.

Transference

First developed by Freud, the notion of transference is that, in analysis, the patient will use the analyst as a screen for his or her fantasies. The analyst may thereby come to stand in for a parent or embody a set of psychic conflicts for the patient.

Transcendent Function

The Jungian transcendent function comes into play when conflicts within the psyche spontaneously produce some powerful symbol that "transcends" the warring forces and so is able to unite them. The transcendent function produces **symbols** that point toward the unknown in the **unconscious**; such **symbols** must not be reduced to words, which are the **ego's** language.

Unconscious

To Jung, the term unconscious denotes both *mental contents inaccessible* to the **ego** and a *psychic arena with its own properties and functions*. The Jungian unconscious is superior to the **ego**, to which it exists in a compensatory relation. It is the locus of meaning, feeling, and value in the psyche. It is *autonomous*, but it is not completely separate from the **body**, rather offering a "third place" between the terms of that perennial duality, **body** and spirit. **Body** and culture influence unconscious contents, but the unconscious is not merely *subject* to either force. The unconscious is structured by **archetypes** as inherited structuring principles.

Visionary Art

Jung divided art into **psychological** and visionary categories. Visionary art consists mainly of **symbols**, which point to what is not yet known or unknowable in the culture. Consequently, visionary art is primarily expressive of the **collective unconscious**. As such it *compensates* the culture for its conscious biases, bringing to **consciousness** what is ignored or repressed. Visionary art may also predict something of the future direction of the culture.

Notes

The major works of C.G. Jung are referred to in the following notes as:

CW   *The Collected Works of C.G. Jung*, Volumes 1 to 18. Trans. R.F.C. Hull, ed. by Sir Herbert Read, Michael Fordham, Gerhard Adler and W. McGuire (Princeton, NJ: Princeton University Press, 1934-1954).

MDR   *Memories, Dreams, Reflections*. Ed. by Aniela Jaffe, trans. Richard and Clara Winston (New York: Random House, 1961).

MMSS   *Modern Man in Search of a Soul*. (London: Routledge and Kegan Paul, 1933).

Chapter 1: Getting Started with Jung

1   Jung, "The Archetypes of the Collective Unconscious," in *The Archetypes of the Collective Unconscious*, CW 9i, § 66.
2   Deirdre Bair, *Jung: A Biography* (New York: Little Brown, 2004), pp. 64-120.
3   *Ibid.*, 109-114.
4   Jung, *MDR*, pp. 217-223.
5   Jung, "On the Nature of the Psyche," in *The Structure and Dynamics of the Psyche*, CW 8, § 417.
6   *Ibid.*, § 358.
7   *Ibid.*, § 545.
8   *Ibid.*, § 702.
9   Jung, "On the Relation of Analytical Psychology to Poetry," in *The Spirit in Man, Art and Literature*, CW 15, § 99.
10 Roger Brooke, *Pathways into the Jungian World: Phenomenology and Analytical Psychology* (London and New York: Routledge, 1999), p. 22.
11 Jung, *MMSS*, pp. 215-216.
12 *Ibid.*, p. 1.
13 *Ibid.*, p. 15.
14 *Ibid.,*, p. 12.
15 *Ibid.*, p. 13.
16 Jung, CW 8, § 389.
17 *Ibid.*
18 *Ibid.*
19 *Ibid.*, § 402.
20 Jung, CW 9i, § 155.
21 Jung, CW 8, § 394.
22 *Ibid.*
23 *Ibid.*, § 381.
24 David Tacey, *How to Read Jung* (London: Granta Books, 2006), pp. 20-21.
25 Jung, CW 9i, § 44.

26   Jung, *MDR*, pp. 210-211.
27   Jung, *CW* 9i, § 64.
28   *Ibid.*, § 29-35.
29   *Ibid.*, § 29.
30   *Ibid.*
31   Jung, *CW* 8, § 849-852.
32   *Ibid.*, § 843-845.
33   *Ibid.*, § 844.
34   *Ibid.*, § 855.
35   *Ibid.*
36   *Ibid.*, § 965.
37   *Ibid.*
38   *Ibid.*, § 858.
39   Jung, *Mysterium Conjunctionis: An Inquiry into the Separation and Synthesis of Psychic Opposites*, in *CW* 14, § 518a.
40   Jung, *CW* 8, § 402.
41   Laurence Coupe, *Myth* (London: Routledge, 1997), pp. 9-35.
42   *Ibid.*, p. 100.
43   Susan Rowland, *Jung: A Feminist Revision* (Cambridge: Polity, 2002).

Chapter 2: Jung the Writer on Psychotherapy and Culture

1   Cited in Bair (2004), p. 336.
2   Jung, *MDR*, p. 160.
3   *Ibid.*, pp. 158-160.
4   Bair (2004), p. 159.
5   *Ibid.*, pp. 332-337.
6   *Ibid.*, p. 337.
7   *Ibid.*, p. 732, n. 37.
8   Jung, *MMSS*, p. 246.
9   Jung, *CW* 8, § 356.
10   Jung, *CW* 15, § 121.
11   Jung, *MMSS*, pp. 215-216.
12   Jung, *Aion: Researches into the Phenomenology of the Self*, *CW* 9ii, § 25.
13   Robert Romanyshyn, *The Wounded Researcher* (New Orleans: Spring Journal Books, 2007).
14   *Ibid.*, pp. 259-307.
15   Jung, *MMSS*, p. 70 and p. 248.
16   *Ibid.*, p. 75.
17   Coupe (1997), p. 9.
18   Jung, *MMSS*, pp. 200-225.
19   *Ibid.*, p. 204.
20   *Ibid.*, pp. 210-211.
21   *Ibid.*, pp. 213.
22   *Ibid.*, pp. 219-220.
23   *Ibid.*, p. 222.
24   *Ibid.*, p. 224.

25 *Ibid.*, pp. 224-225.
26 *Ibid.*, p. 225.
27 *Ibid.*, pp. 226-254.
28 *Ibid.*, pp. 226-228.
29 *Ibid.*, pp. 227-228.
30 *Ibid.*, p. 230.
31 *Ibid.*, p. 231.
32 *Ibid.*, p. 233.
33 *Ibid.*, pp. 235-236.
34 *Ibid.*, p. 242.
35 *Ibid.*
36 *Ibid.*, p. 246.
37 *Ibid.*
38 *Ibid.*, p. 248.
39 *Ibid.*, p. 249.
40 *Ibid.*, pp. 253-254.
41 *Ibid.*, p. 254.

Chapter 3: Jung for Literature, Art, and Film

1   Bair (2004), pp. 301-303 and 405-407.
2   James Joyce, *Ulysses* (New York: Penguin, 1922/1992).
3   Jung, "*Ulysses*: a Monologue," in *The Spirit in Man, Art and Literature, CW* 15.
4   *Ibid.*, § 169.
5   *Ibid.*, § 184.
6   *Ibid.*, § 178.
7   *Ibid.*, § 201.
8   Jung, *CW* 15, § 97-132.
9   *Ibid.*, § 121.
10 Jane Austen, *Mansfield Park* (New York: Penguin, 1814/2000).
11 Emily Brontë, *Wuthering Heights* (New York: Penguin, 1848/1998).
12 Jung, "Psychology and Literature," in *The Spirit in Man, Art and Literature*, *CW* 15, § 139.
13 *Ibid.*, § 141.
14 Edward Saïd, *Culture and Imperialism* (New York: Random House, 1993), pp. 80-96.
15 Diana M.A. Relke, *Greenwor(l)ds: Ecocritical Readings of Canadian Women's Poetry* (Calgary: University of Calgary Press, 1999), pp. 11-38.
16 Edmund Cusick, "Psyche and the Artist: Jung and the Poet," in *Psyche and the Arts: Jungian Approaches to Music, Architecture, Literature, Painting and Film*, edited by Susan Rowland (London and New York: Routledge, 2008), pp. 12-21.
17 Don Fredericksen, "Jung/Sign/Symbol/Film," in Christopher Hauke and Ian Alister, eds., *Jung and Film: Post-Jungian Takes on the Moving Image* (London and New York: Routledge, 2001), pp. 17-55.
18 See Annis Pratt, *Archetypal Patterns in Women's Fiction* (Indiana: Indiana University Press, 184) and Bettina Knapp, *Women in Twentieth Century Literature: A Jungian View* (Pennsylvania: Pennsylvania State University Press, 1987).
19 John Beebe, "The Trickster in the Arts," *San Francisco Jung Institute Library Journal*, vol. 2, no. 2 (1981): 48.

20 Terrie Waddell, *Mis/Takes: Archetype, Myth and Identity in Screen Fiction* (London and New York: Routledge, 2006).

21 John Izod, *Screen, Culture, Psyche: A Post-Jungian Approach to Working with the Audience* (London and New York: Routledge, 2006).

22 Terence Dawson, *The Effective Protagonist in the Nineteenth-Century British Novel: Scott, Brontë, Eliot, Wilde* (London: Ashgate, 2004).

23 See Susan Rowland, "Jung and Derrida: the Numinous, Deconstruction and Myth," in Ann Casement and David Tacey, eds., *The Idea of the Numinous: Contemporary Jungian and Psychoanalytic Perspectives* (London: Taylor and Francis, 2006), pp. 98-116.

24 Izod (2006), p. 6.

25 Luke Hockley, *Frames of Mind: A Post-Jungian Look at Film, Television and Technology* (London and New York: Routledge, 2007).

26 Luke Hockley, "Film Noir: Archetypes or Stereotypes?" in Hauke and Alister (2001), pp. 177-193.

27 Izod (2006), p. 18.

28 *Ibid.*, p. 19.

29 Susan Rowland, *C.G. Jung and Literary Theory: The Challenge from Fiction* (London: Palgrave, 1999).

30 See Susan Rowland (2006), pp. 98-116.

31 Don Fredericksen, "Jung/Sign/Symbol/Film," in Hauke and Alister (2001), pp. 17-55.

32 Don Fredericksen, *Bergman's Persona* (Poznan: Wydawnictwo Naukowe, 2005).

33 Don Fredericksen, "Stripping Bare the Images," in Rowland (2008), p. 101.

34 Joseph Campbell, *The Hero with a Thousand Faces* (Princeton, NJ: Princeton University Press, 1949).

35 Christopher Vogler, *The Writer's Journey: Mythic Structure for Writers* (Studio City, CA: Michael Wiese Productions, 1997/2007).

36 Don Williams, ""If You Could See What I've Seen With Your Eyes…": Post-Human Psychology and *Blade Runner*," in Hauke and Alister (2001), pp. 110-128.

Chapter 4: Myth and History

1   The full tragic story is well documented in the correspondence between Freud and Jung. See Sigmund Freud and C.G. Jung, *The Freud/Jung Letters*, ed. William McGuire, trans. R.F.C. Hull (Princeton, NJ: Princeton University Press, 1994).

2   Jung, *MDR*.

3   *Ibid.*, pp. 194-195.

4   *Ibid.*

5   Rowland (2002), pp. 21-45.

6   Seamus Heaney, *Opened Ground: Poems 1966-96* (London: Faber and Faber, 1998), pp. 455-456.

7   Coupe (1997), pp. 9-35.

8   *Ibid.*, p. 105.

9   *Ibid.*, pp. 100-115.

10 *Ibid.*, p. 103.

11 Ann Baring and Jules Cashford, *The Myth of the Goddess: Evolution of an Image* (London and New York: Penguin Arkana, 1993).

12 Campbell (1949).

13   Lynn White Jr., "The Historical Roots of our Ecologic Crisis," in Cheryll Glotfelty and Harold Fromm, eds., *The Ecocriticism Reader: Landmarks in Literary Ecology* (Athens and London: The University of Georgia Press, 1996), pp. 3-14.

14   Ursula K. Le Guin, "The Carrier Bag Theory of Fiction," in Glotfelty and Fromm (1996), pp. 149-154.

15   Jung, "Answer to Job," in *Psychology and Religion: West and East, CW* 11.

16   William Shakespeare, *The Tempest*, ed. by Virginia Mason (London: The Arden Shakespeare, 1611/1999).

17   Jung, *CW* 9ii.

18   *Ibid.*, § 150.

19   *Ibid.*

20   Shakespeare (1611/1999), Act V Sc. 1, lines 273-274.

Chapter 5: Jung and Science, Alchemy, and Religion

1   Jung, *MDR*, pp. 104-5.

2   Jung, *CW* 9ii, § 208.

3   Jung, *MDR*, pp. 55-57.

4   *Ibid.*, pp. 150-152.

5   Francis Bacon was a philosopher, scientist, and lawyer whose inductive method of scientific inquiry has proven enormously influential up until the present day.

6   René Descartes was a French philosopher and mathematician who spent much of his life in the Dutch Republic. Descartes is famous for his declaration, *Cogito ergo sum* ("I think, therefore I am" or "I am thinking, therefore I exist").

7   Isaac Newton described gravitation for the first time, and formulated the Three Laws of Motion, which became the dominant paradigm for physics until the twentieth century. He also delineated the light spectrum and optics.

8   Francis Bacon, *Novum Organum*, trans. and ed. by Peter Urbach and John Gibson (Illinois: Carus, Open Court, 1994).

9   René Descartes, *Discourse on Method* (London: Everyman Paperbacks, 1637/1994).

10   Isaac Newton, *Philosophiae Natralis Principia Mathematica*, trans. I. Bernard Cohen and Anne Whitman (Berkeley and Los Angeles: University of California Press, 1687/1999).

11   Jung, *CW* 15, § 121.

12   Jung, *CW* 8, § 343-442.

13   *Ibid.*, § 358.

14   *Ibid.*, § 421.

15   Jung, *CW* 12.

16   *Ibid.*, § 420.

17   *Ibid.*, § 432.

18   *Ibid.*, § 305.

19   *Ibid.*

20   *Ibid.*, § 498.

21   *Ibid.*, § 377-394.

22   *Ibid.*, § 394.

23   Roderick Main, *The Rupture of Time: Synchronicity and Jung's Critique of Modern Western Culture* (London and New York: Brunner-Routledge, 2004).

24   Jung, *MMSS*, pp. 143-174.

25   Jung, "Synchronicity: An Acausal Connecting Principle," in *The Structure and Dynamics of the Psyche, CW* 8, § 843.
26   *Ibid.*, § 864.
27   *Ibid.*, § 965.
28   Jung, *CW* 15, § 105.
29   Jung, *CW* 12, § 394, 400.
30   *Ibid.*, § 400.
31   Jung, *CW* 11, § 553-758.
32   *Ibid.*, § 745.
33   *Ibid.*, § 733.

Chapter 6: Jung and Power: Politics and Gender

1   See especially Andrew Samuels, *The Political Psyche* (London and New York: Routledge, 1993) and *Politics on the Couch: Citizenship and the Internal Life* (London: Profile Books, 2001).
2   See also Rowland (2002) for more on Jung, gender, and feminism.
3   Samuels (1993), pp. 292-294.
4   Bair (2004), p. 459.
5   Samuels (1993), pp. 292-294.
6   *Ibid.*, pp. 292-294.
7   Jung, "The State of Psychotherapy Today," in *Civilization in Transition, CW* 10.
8   Samuels (1993), pp. 292-293.
9   *Ibid.*, p. 293.
10   *Ibid.*
11   *Ibid.*
12   Bair (2004), pp. 448-450.
13   *Ibid.*, 459.
14   *Ibid.*
15   *Ibid.*, pp. 486-495.
16   *Ibid.*, p. 492.
17   Samuels (1993), pp. 305-311.
18   *Ibid.*, p. 311.
19   Samuels (2001), pp. 64-74.
20   *Ibid.*, p. 66.
21   *Ibid.*, p. 67.
22   Susan Rowland, *Jung as a Writer* (London and New York: Routledge, 2005), pp. 196-211.
23   William Shakespeare, *Hamlet*, ed. by Neil Taylor and Ann Thompson (London: Arden, 1601/2006).
24   Bair (2004), pp. 108-123, 145-158.
25   *Ibid.*, p. 266
26   *Ibid.*, p. 265.
27   *Ibid.*, pp. 264-267.
28   *CW* 9ii, § 29
29   Jung, "Marriage as a Psychological Relationship," in *The Development of Personality, CW* 17, § 338.
30   Jung, *MDR*, pp. 210-211.

31   Jung, "On the Psychology and Pathology of so-Called Occult Phenomena," in *Psychiatric Studies*, *CW* 17, § 1-150.

32   F.X. Charet, *Spiritualism and the Foundations of C. G. Jung's Psychology* (New York: State University of New York Press, 1993).

33   Jung, *CW* 17, § 97.

34   *Ibid.*, § 65-6.

35   James Hillman, "Anima," in *Spring: An Annual of Archetypal Psychology and Jungian Thought* (New York: Spring Publications, 1973): 97-132; "Anima (II)," in *Spring: An Annual of Archetypal Psychology and Jungian Thought* (New York: Spring Publications, 1974): 113-146.

36   Ginette Paris, *Pagan Meditations: Aphrodite, Hestia, Artemis* (Woodstock, CT: Spring Publications Inc., 1986).

37   Ginette Paris, *Wisdom of the Psyche* (London and New York: Routledge, 2007).

Chapter 7: Jung in the Twenty-First Century: Fishing at the Gates of Hell

1   Jung, *MDR*, pp. 320-323.

2   Jung, *CW* 11.

3   Jung, *Psychology and Alchemy*, *CW* 12, § 182.

4   Jung, "On the Psychology of the Trickster Figure," in *The Archetypes of the Collective Unconscious*, *CW* 9i, § 456-488.

5   *Ibid.*, § 479.

6   *Ibid.*

7   Jung, *CW* 9ii.

8   *Ibid.*, § 192.

9   *Ibid.*, § 191.

10   *Ibid.*, § 202.

11   *Ibid.*, § 206.

12   *Ibid.*, § 209.

13   *Ibid.*

14   *Ibid.*

15   David L. Miller, *Hell and Holy Ghosts: A Theopoetics of Christian Belief* (New Orleans: Spring Journal Books, 2004).

16   See Baring and Cashford (1993), especially Chapter 3.

17   Thomas S. Kuhn, *The Structure of Scientific Revolutions* (Chicago: University of Chicago Press, 1962/1996).

18   James Lovelock, *Gaia: A New Look at Life on Earth* (Oxford: Oxford University Press, 1979).

19   Wendy Wheeler, *The Whole Creature: Complexity, Biosemiotics and the Evolution of Culture* (London: Lawrence and Wishart, 2006).

20   Jerome Bernstein, *Living in the Borderland: the Evolution of Consciousness and the Challenge of Healing Trauma* (London and New York: Routledge, 2005).

21   Joseph Cambray, "Synchronicity as Emergence," in Joseph Cambray and Linda Carter, eds., *Analytical Psychology: Contemporary Perspectives in Jungian Analysis* (London and New York: Routledge, 2004).

22   Wheeler (2006), p. 47.

23   Bernstein (2005).

24   Richard Tarnas, *Cosmos and Psyche: Intimations of a New World View* (New York: Viking, 2006).

25   *Ibid.*, p. 489.

26   Roger Brooke, *Jung and Phenomenology* (London and New York: Routledge, 1991), and also his edited collection, *Pathways into the Jungian World: Phenomenology and Analytical Psychology* (London and New York: Routledge, 1999).

27   Roger Brooke, in *Encyclopedia of Psychology and Religion,* ed. by David Leeming, Kathryn Madden and Stanton Marlan (New York: Springer, 2010), http://www.springer.com/psychology/psychology+general/book/978-0-387-71802-6.

28   Jung, *CW* 8.

29   See Rowland (2005), Chapter 4 on "On the Nature of the Psyche," pp. 70-99.

30   Robert Romanyshyn, *The Wounded Researcher* (New Orleans: Spring Journal Books, 2007).

31   Lee Worth Bailey, *The Enchantments of Technology* (Urbana and Chicago: University of Illinois Press, 2005).

32   Jung, *CW* 9ii, § 368.

33   Bailey (2005), p. 17.

34   Ronald Schenk, *The Sunken Quest, The Wasted Fisher, The Pregnant Fish: Postmodern Reflections on Depth Psychology* (Wilmette Illinois: Chiron, 2001).

35   *Ibid.*, p. 15.

36   T. S. Eliot, "The Wasteland," in Margaret Ferguson, Mary Jo Salter and Jon Stallworthy, eds., *The Norton Anthology of Poetry* (New York and London: W.W. Norton, 1922/2005), p. 1344.

37   Schenk (2001), p. 146.

38   Joel Weishaus, "The Way North," http://www.cddc.vt.edu/host/weishaus/North/Intro.htm.

39   *Ibid.*

Index

A

Enlightenment, the 22, 31, 38, 39, 105, 111
epic poetry 62
eros/eros consciousness 13–14, 88, 89, 133, 138, 139, 154, 155, 163, 164, 178, 179
Eros (Greek god) 141–142
essentialism/anti-essentialism 66, 68, 89, 133
Europe 28, 29, 31, 34, 35, 41, 78, 92, 93, 150–151
  sickness of 51
European consciousness 92
Eurydice 162, 168
evil 147, 149, 151, 182
  and trickster figure 65
Excalibur (Boorman) 62, 75
Eyes Wide Shut (Kubrick) 67

F

fairy tales 164
fantasy
  power of 104
father 180. *See also* Sky Father
feminine 2, 5, 94, 116, 132, 140, 153–154, 182
  as image (Hillman) 142
  as Other 137, 142
  devaluation of the 134, 140
  myths of the 85
  as narrative (Paris) 142
  power of 5
  voice of 137
feminism 123, 140, 145, 153
Feminism and the Mastery of Nature (Plumwood) 26
film
  commercial 67
  symbolism 69
"Film Noir: Archetypes or Stereotypes?" (Hockley) 73
Fink, Dr. Cary 29
fish, fishing 165, 166
Fool 149, 150
founding myths of consciousness 2
Fowles, John 62
fractals 155
Fredericksen, Don 63, 67, 68–70, 72–73
"free association" (Freudian technique) 4
Freud, Sigmund 3, 4, 8, 11, 27, 28–29, 52, 77, 90–91, 97, 109, 124, 125, 127, 128, 131, 136, 137, 140, 180
  fainting incident with Jung 78–81, 90
"future history" 92–93

G

Gaia: A New Look at Life on Earth (Lovelock) 172
Gaia hypothesis 155
gender 12–13, 59, 85, 89, 115, 117, 123, 132–135, 137, 140–143, 145, 175, 176, 181
  the unconscious and 133–134
gender bias 134, 141
gender fluidity 134, 141
gender studies 123
Genesis, Book of 116, 138, 153, 158
Germany 123, 143
global warming 167
Gnosticism 40, 92, 163
God 115, 149–150, 151. *See also* Sky Father
  as clockmaker 106
  consciousness of 149
  dark side of 103, 119–120, 149
  in *Hamlet* 130
  and Job 119
  as separate from matter/physical universe 112, 116, 153
  the unconscious as 102
goddess. *See* Earth Mother/goddess
Golden Gate Bridge 164
Göring, Matthias 124
Great Mother 8. *See also* Earth Mother/goddess
Greece/Greeks, ancient 21, 33, 34, 78, 82, 141, 142, 179
Greek mythology 9, 141
green lion (alchemical symbol) 113
Green Studies Reader, The (Coupe) 26

H

Hamlet (Shakespeare) 65, 129–132
  audience's role in 130–131
Handbook of Jungian Psychology, The (Papadopoulos) 25
Hauke, Christopher 73, 171
healing 6
Heaney, Seamus 81, 82, 83, 99
Heaven 151
Hell 151, 172
  as fear of death 168
  in the North 151–154, 168
  as underworld 168
Hells and Holy Ghosts (Miller) 152, 172
Heraclitus 24
hermeneutic circle 160, 163

R

S

W

Z